115 COUNTRY INNS
of
New Hampshire & Vermont

DOWN EAST BOOKS / CAMDEN, MAINE

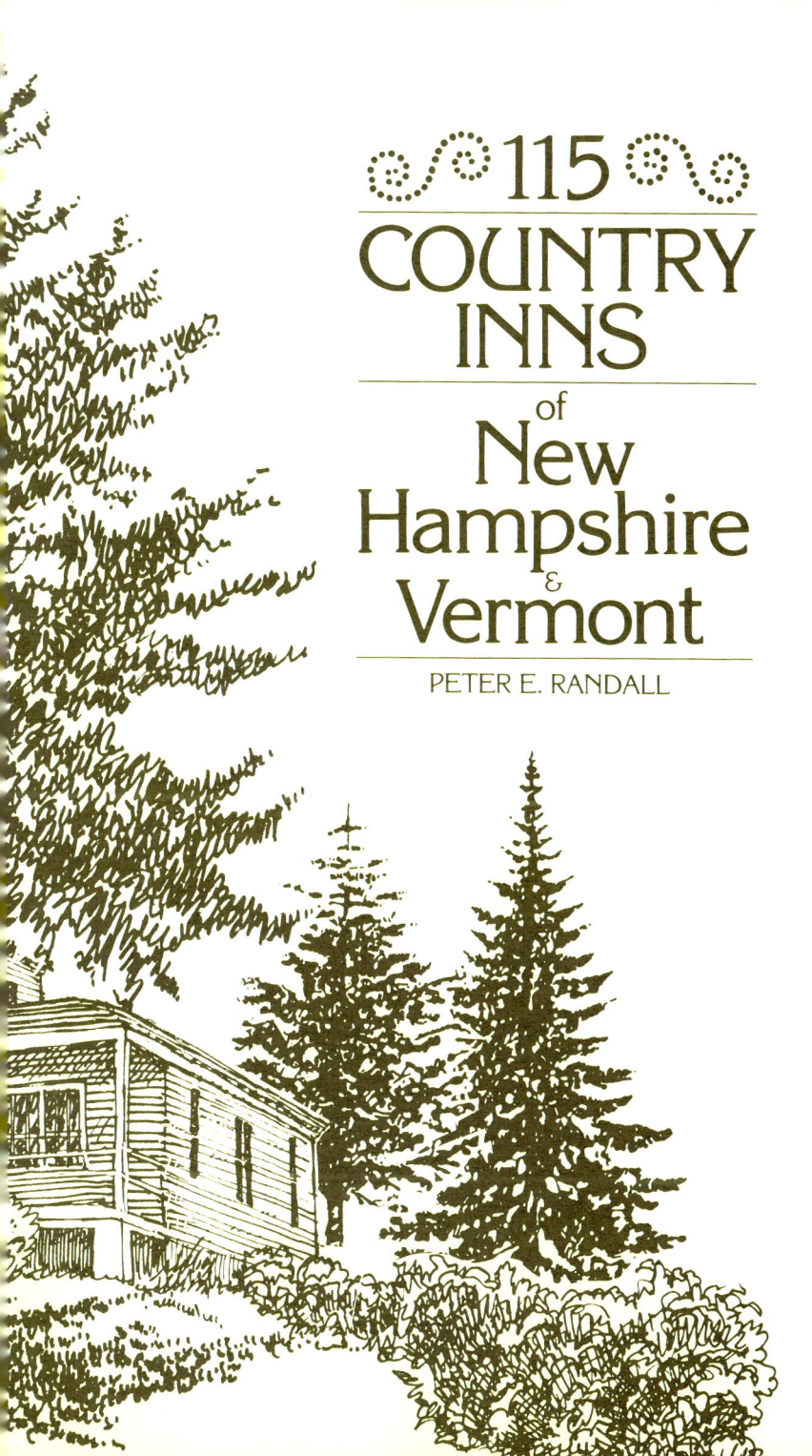

115 COUNTRY INNS
of New Hampshire & Vermont

PETER E. RANDALL

Copyright 1982 by Peter E. Randall

ISBN 0-89272-141-3

Library of Congress Catalogue Card Number 81-70941

Cover illustration: Lawrence Zwart

Design: Lurelle Cheverie

Composition: The Offset House

Printed in the United States of America

DOWN EAST BOOKS CAMDEN, MAINE 04843

CONTENTS

Introduction   vii

A Guide for the Inn Visitor   xi

NEW HAMPSHIRE   1

VERMONT   109

Index of Inns   257

INTRODUCTION

"Were I to form a picture of a happy society, it would be a town consisting of a due mixture of hills, valleys and streams of water: The land well fenced and cultivated; the roads and bridges in good repair; a decent inn for the refreshment of travellers, and for public entertainments. . . ."

The Reverend Jeremy Belknap wrote those words nearly two hundred years ago in his three-volume *History of New Hampshire*. He would be pleased today to learn that inns have again become important institutions in many small New Hampshire and Vermont towns.

The current revival of interest in country inns might well have been expected. After all, the traveling public can be satisfied with chain motels and franchise restaurants for only so long. But there are other reasons for the comeback of the country inn. In the past they were used by people who were traveling to a destination but now many inns have become the destination itself. Guests come to an inn to dine graciously, sleep comfortably, and spend their days reading, antiquing, bicycling, or enjoying a winter sport.

Many inns require their guests to provide their own entertainment, and it is interesting how easily people make new friends and how quickly they forget television, daily newspapers, and ringing telephones.

The inns are popular because each one is different. Building sizes, shapes, and ages vary considerably. Methods of operation change from inn to inn because each one is a small independent business and the owners bring their own individual ideas to their inn.

One owner told me there are really two rules of innkeeping: first, you can't be a native, and second, you must never have run an inn before. While these "rules" might spell disaster in some businesses — and do, in fact, doom an inn or two every year — some of the best inns we visited were run by people who had tired of another lifestyle or career and decided to try innkeeping.

For those who don't already know it, innkeeping is difficult work. Days beginning at 7 A.M. and ending after midnight are commonplace. Often there is little free time to spend with spouse or children. Repairs, new equipment, and rising costs of operation often seem overwhelming. Too much rain in summer and too little snow in winter have an impact on the innkeeper just as they do on the farmer or ski area.

Nevertheless, many inns remain under the same management for years, and sometimes children take over from their parents. Other inns change hands regularly until someone comes along with the right combination of money, talent, and temperament to make a success where others have failed.

Jeremy Belknap would have approved of that circumstance, too.

We believe there are three types of inns. First comes the true village inn as mentioned by Belknap. Located in the middle of a village, perhaps on the common or green, it often is the focus of social life in the community, where you can have a drink in the bar with locals and visitors from the city. The general store will be nearby, and you can sit and rock on the front porch and get a glimpse of America the way most old-timers remember it. Village inns usually have a public dining room with a varied menu, sometimes traditional and often continental, and many have been serving the public for a hundred years or more.

The rural inn is likely to be off the main road, is usually smaller than its village cousin, and caters mainly to travelers who come for several days' vacation in the country. Often the inn is a converted farmhouse, dinner may be a one-entrée continental feast, and the activities are slower paced.

The third type of inn is more accurately a fine restaurant with some rooms for overnight guests and few other amenities.

Many inns in this book fit nicely into one of these three categories while others combine elements of two or all three. We have attempted to describe each inn accurately so that choices can be made depending on your mood or reason for visiting an inn.

In selecting the inns in this volume — and we visited some 140 places — we had several criteria. First, the inn had to serve at least one meal, even if only a full breakfast, but not just a continental breakfast. The inn had to be housed in an old building and, in fact, most we visited were built in the 19th century and a few in the 18th century. A couple date from the 1940s. The inns we selected are small, most under twenty rooms. We believe that some of the large inns, despite their historical traditions, are more like hotels or resorts and we have not included them here.

All the information given here is accurate as of the time of publication, but the fortunes of the inn business are always subject to change, and there are a few places we couldn't visit in time to review them for this book. We plan to update the book periodically, though, and we welcome comments or suggestions about the inns listed or those missing.

Letters may be sent to:
Editor, New Hampshire & Vermont Inns
Down East Books
P.O. Box 679
Camden, ME 04843

A GUIDE FOR THE INN VISITOR

Rates: MAP is modified American plan and includes breakfast, dinner, and lodging.

EP is European plan with lodging only but sometimes a continental breakfast. Dinner or full breakfast is extra.

B & B is bed and breakfast.

All rates in this book are listed for two people sharing one room per night. Rates for singles are somewhat more than half the amount listed. Please realize that rates change; if you are reading this book several seasons after the date of publication, expect to pay somewhat more for accommodations.

Gratuity and Taxes. Both New Hampshire and Vermont have rooms and meals taxes and these amounts will be added to bills. Many inns automatically add a 10-15 percent gratuity to the bill.

Reservations. Always call ahead for reservations. Most of these inns are small and they fill quickly for holidays or peak seasons such as foliage time. Always confirm rates and inquire about any special features that we have mentioned here. Inns and innkeepers change, and that special menu might not be exactly as listed here.

Deposits. Expect to send a deposit usually within a week to confirm your reservations. Most inns want at least a deposit equal to one night's stay, and during certain weekends or seasons some inns require a two or three night reservation. Usually the inns will return most of your deposit if you have to cancel two weeks to ten days before your planned arrival. Some will return most of the deposit even on shorter notice if the room can be rented to someone else. Remember that the inns are small and the loss of one room's income is important. If you think you might have to cancel, inquire about the inn's policy.

Children and Pets. A few inns don't accept either children or pets and many inns take children over a certain age only. Most old inns are not soundproof, and the noise of one crying infant can keep the whole place awake. Also, many couples visit inns to get away from jobs or families. Inns with these restrictions usually don't have much for children to do anyway so it is best to seek out those places which welcome families. Many are listed here. Pets are welcome in a few inns, usually by prior arrangement. Don't show up unannounced with your great dane and expect a red carpet treatment. Many inns can recommend a nearby kennel for your pet.

Charge Cards. We've listed many inns that don't take any charge cards but are happy to accept cash or personal checks. Even inns that do handle Visa, Mastercharge, Diner's Club or American Express appreciate cash or checks. If you do travel with plastic, make sure your destination accepts your cards.

Shared Baths. These are a fact of life in most inns although often there is one bath for every two rooms. Usually there is no problem getting your turn, and if the one across the hall is busy then try the one down the hall. Some inns now supply terry cloth robes for those using shared baths.

One advantage: Rooms with shared baths are usually priced $10-20 less per night.

Seasons. We originally planned to list only inns open most of the year but that would have eliminated many fine places, and we later learned that several inns formerly open all year are now closing in the winter. Most inns are open May through October and from December to the end of ski season. Some inns that are open all year have reduced services in slow periods. We believe that May, early June, September, late October, and winter mid-week periods are great times to visit inns. The weather is still nice but business is slower then, and you'll often have a choice of rooms.

Liquor. Most inns have liquor licenses and many have fine wine lists. Innkeepers love to discuss their wines, and they will be happy to recommend a variety, vintage, and price to suit you. Inns without liquor licenses allow guests to bring their own beverages and most will keep bottles cold in the refrigerator and provide setups before and after dinner.

Inn-to-Inn and Exercise. After visiting inns for six months we sorely needed some exercise. Dinners and breakfasts are always more than ample. One fine way to keep fit and still enjoy inn hopping is bicycling. In Vermont several outfitters and tour guides package weekend (and longer) bike trips, and most use inns for overnight stops.

We learned about the following:

Vermont Country Cyclers
Box 148
Waterbury Center, VT 04677

Vermont Bicycle Touring
RD #3
Bristol, VT 05443

Bike Vermont
Box 75
Grafton, VT 05146

Typically these businesses provide planned itineraries, rent bikes, some offer discounts for people arriving by public transportation, and most operate from May to

October. Most have guides with each group and vans to carry bags, make repairs, or assist those who get tired.

Ski Tours of Vermont, RFD 1, Chester, VT 05143 offers guided ski tours. Mike Shonstrom, Churchill House, RFD #3, Brandon, VT 05733 will package inn-to-inn tours for bikers, hikers, skiers, canoeists, fishermen, and about any other type of traveler. The Stone House, N. Thetford, VT 05054 conducts canoe trips on the Connecticut River.

In New Hampshire, any of the Jackson area inns will assist with inn-to-inn cross-country ski tours.

NEW HAMPSHIRE

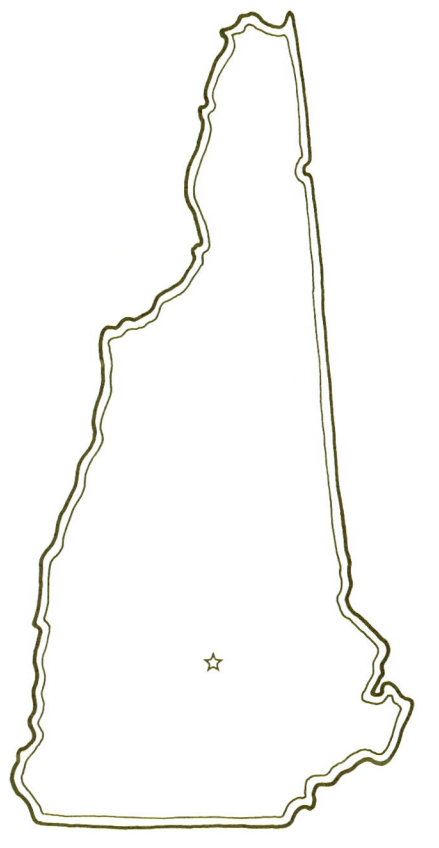

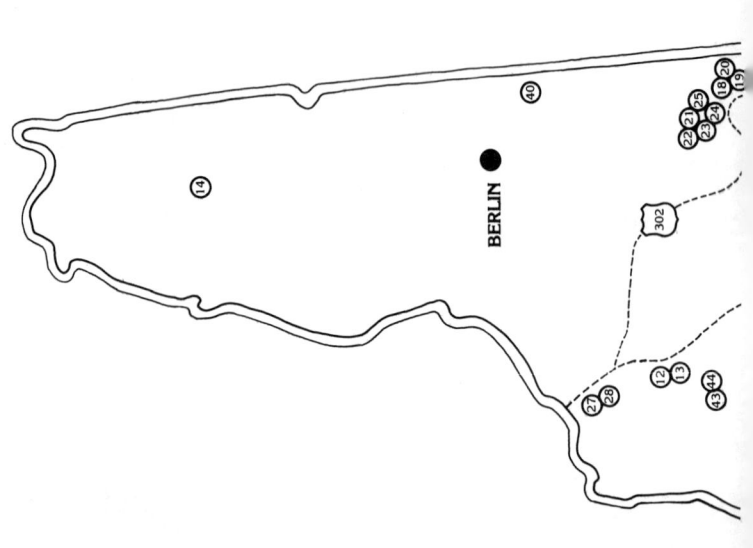

New Hampshire

1 **ANTRIM** Maplehurst Inn
2 **BRADFORD** The Bradford Inn
3 **BRIDGEWATER** Pasquaney Inn
4 **CAMPTON VILLAGE** The Village Guest House
5 **CENTER SANDWICH** The Corner House Inn
6 **CHOCORUA** Staffords-in-the-Fields
7 **CONWAY** Darby Field Inn
8 **EATON CENTER** Palmer House Inn
9 **EATON CENTER** Rock House Mountain Farm
10 **FITZWILLIAM** Fitzwilliam Inn
11 **FRANCESTOWN** Inn at Crotched Mountain
12 **FRANCONIA** The Horse and Hound Inn

13 FRANCONIA Lovett's by Lafayette Brook
14 GLEN The Bernerhof Inn and Restaurant
15 GOSHEN The Back Side Inn
16 HANCOCK John Hancock Inn
17 HENNIKER Colby Hill Inn
18 INTERVALE Holiday Inn
19 INTERVALE The New England Inn
20 INTERVALE Tuckerman's Inn and Tavern
21 JACKSON Christmas Farm Inn
22 JACKSON Dana Place Inn
23 JACKSON Whitneys' Village Inn
24 JACKSON VILLAGE Thorn Hill Lodge
25 JACKSON VILLAGE Wildcat Inn and Tavern
26 JAFFREY CENTER Monadnock Inn
27 LITTLETON Beal House Inn
28 LITTLETON Edencroft Manor
29 LYME The Lyme Inn
30 MILFORD The Ram in the Thicket
31 NEW LONDON Hide-Away Lodge
32 NEW LONDON New London Inn
33 NEW LONDON Pleasant Lake Inn
34 NORTH CHARLESTOWN Indian Shutters Inn
35 NORTH CONWAY Cranmore Mountain Lodge
36 NORTH CONWAY Stonehurst Manor
37 NORTH SUTTON Follansbee Inn
38 PORTSMOUTH The Inn at Christian Shore
39 PORTSMOUTH Martin Hill Inn
40 SHELBURNE Philbrook Farm Inn
41 SNOWVILLE Snowvillage Inn
42 STODDARD CENTER Pitcher Mountain Inn
43 SUGAR HILL The Homestead
44 SUGAR HILL Sunset Hill House
45 SUNAPEE Dexter's Inn
46 TAMWORTH Tamworth Inn
47 TEMPLE Birchwood Inn

Maplehurst Inn

Route 202

ANTRIM, NEW HAMPSHIRE 03440

Telephone: 603-588-2891

Innkeeper: Jerry Wright

Maplehurst has been serving travelers since 1794 although we suspect that its menu has never been quite so interesting as it is now under the direction of chef Jerry Wright. All the food from appetizers to desserts is prepared on the premises and all vegetables are fresh, none canned or frozen. Breakfast is served to guests only, but the public is welcome for dinner. The dinner menu ranges from beef Wellington and coquille St. Jacques to filet of sole and deep dish chicken pie.

Eight of sixteen rooms have private baths, with the other rooms sharing two baths. The rooms are well-furnished but not fancy, as befits an older inn. The beds are mostly old with various combinations of twins and doubles. A few rooms have television. There is a rustic tavern on the main floor. The three dining rooms seat seventy-five people, and one room has a fireplace.

Antrim is a small town, and the inn is prominent on the main street next to the First Presbyterian Church and just across from the brick town hall. Several ski areas are only a short drive away.

Jerry says he wants to keep this as a country inn. Is he successful? Ask Walter Cronkite. He's been a guest several times.

Open all year. Charge cards, liquor license. The inn is on Route 202, midway between Peterborough and Hillsborough.

ACCOMMODATIONS: EP $20 - $35
                  Dinner $6 - $13

The Bradford Inn

Main Street

BRADFORD, NEW HAMPSHIRE 03221

Telephone: 603-938-5309

Innkeepers: Tom and Woody Best

A village inn has been in this same location since the 1800s. This particular building was completed in 1891 and has been serving the public ever since.

Tom is the chef, specializing in New England home-style cooking with his own lobster Newburg, beef and wine, and custom cut sirloin as menu highlights. The Bests make their own breads, soups, desserts, pickles, and relishes. All of the entrées are cooked to order and are served in the large dining room which is open to the public by reservation. The Bests added the restaurant and a small lounge to the facility when they came five years ago. The lounge has a fireplace and easy chairs. Occasionally musical entertainment is offered.

The inn has twelve rooms, eight with private baths, and three suites with private baths and sitting rooms. Rooms are furnished with double and twin beds and furnishings are typical New England country style. The upstairs halls are quite wide, with easy chairs and plenty of books and magazines about.

Bradford is primarily a quiet country village, but several state parks, ski areas, and lakes are nearby for those in need of a more energetic weekend.

Open all year. Credit cards, liquor license. From exit 9 on I-89 follow Route 103 to Bradford and turn west at the lights onto Main Street and the inn.

ACCOMMODATIONS: *MAP* two or more days on request, $70.
EP from $30

Pasquaney Inn

BRIDGEWATER, NEW HAMPSHIRE 03222

Telephone: 603-744-2712

Innkeepers: Marge and Roy Zimmer

With the sun setting over Mt. Cardigan in the distance, we can't imagine a better place to spend the late afternoon than sitting on one of the long porches of Pasquaney Inn and watching sailboats on Newfound Lake, one of New England's clearest and cleanest.

This is a family-oriented inn with special rates for families and half-price meals for the children. A huge barn behind the inn is a total recreation area for young people with many games, shuffleboard and even basketball (we said it was a *huge* barn). A fine beach on the lake, just across the street from the inn, also has rowboats and a dock. Sailboats can be rented nearby. For those needing more exercise, a walk to the summit of Cardigan offers a commanding view of central New Hampshire.

The inn has twenty-eight rooms in two adjoining buildings. The inn has been completely redecorated and refurnished. There are extra chairs in each room and braided rugs. Some rooms have private baths, but most of the rest have one shared bath for two rooms.

Marge plans the menu and usually two entrées are offered nightly. Toddler's meals are available and those on special diets are accommodated.

Dinner begins with an unusual soup such as dill pickle, broccoli, or perhaps clam chowder, followed by salad and homemade bread or rolls. Entrées include roast duck with orange sauce, London broil or steak au poivre, and stuffed filet of sole. Homemade desserts include parfaits. The inn serves its own fresh vegetables. Box lunches are provided on twenty-four hour notice.

The large sitting room has plenty of books and a piano where guests often provide their own after-dinner music. As a special treat, the inn has a bicycle built for two, but to use it you must be eighteen and in love!

Open May to mid-October, mid-November to March. Liquor license, children. From exit 23 on I-93, follow Route 104 west to Bristol, then take Route 3A north to the lake and the inn.

ACCOMMODATIONS: *EP* from $46
                                         MAP from $76

Village Guest House

Box 222, Route 175

CAMPTON VILLAGE, NEW HAMPSHIRE 03223

Telephone: 603-726-4449

Innkeepers: John DiGiovanni and Marie St. Hilaire

This unusual inn is a welcome addition to the lodging institutions in the Campton-Waterville Valley area. Most overnight accommodations in the region are circa 1930s or modern motels. Good beds perhaps, but not the type of place that inn hoppers are seeking.

The Village Guest House fills the void. Situated right in Campton Village, it is away from the hustle of the ski crowd or summer tourist, yet it is just a few minutes from Waterville Valley. This 1825 farmhouse has ten rooms, two rooms each sharing a modern bath. Although a few of the rooms are a bit small, they are well furnished with old comfortable beds and other antiques.

Heated primarily with a large woodstove in the parlor, the inn also has a large fireplace in the lounge area.

John is the breakfast cook, serving fresh home-baked breads, eggs, slab bacon, hot cereals, waffles, and pancakes. Dinners are cooked on request.

Store skis or bikes in the small barn. Cross-country trails begin in the back yard.

Open all year. BYOB. From exit 28 on I-93, travel toward Waterville Valley and turn left at the lights at the junction of Route 175. The inn is on the corner of Owl Street and Route 175.

ACCOMMODATIONS: *EP* $24 - $32

The Corner House Inn

CENTER SANDWICH, NEW HAMPSHIRE 03227

Telephone: 603-284-6219

Innkeepers: Jane Kroeger and Don Brown

Center Sandwich is one of New Hampshire's prettiest villages and with this hundred-year-old inn under new ownership and again offering lodging, travelers can enjoy the town for more than just a day trip.

This inn is now an offshoot of the nearby and popular Common Man and Woodshed restaurants where Jane and Don have nine years of experience. Lunch and dinner are served daily, with breakfast for house guests only. The menu is quite varied, ranging from chicken Kiev and fettucini Alfredo to shrimp scampi and inn pie made with seafood, poultry, or beef. Salads, crepes, and a wide selection of gourmet sandwiches are offered for lunch. Don't forget to save room for homemade desserts.

Center Sandwich is a dry town, so BYOB, and the bartender will store your beverage and make your drinks during dinner.

There are four dining rooms, but our favorite is in the restored barn, with its old beams and woodstove with soup pot. Most of the inn, including the barn, is decorated with original works of art by local craftspeople. Some items are for sale and others are part of the owner's collection. If you come with a group, you can select one of the smaller dining rooms. Candlelight and antiques create the perfect country atmosphere.

The inn has four bedrooms, one with private bath, all freshly decorated and furnished with antiques and older pieces.

Center Sandwich is a village of white houses and fences with many artists, antique shops, and a fine historical society museum all within walking distance of the inn. The popular Sandwich County Fair is held each Columbus Day.

Open all year. Charge cards, children, BYOB. From exit 23 on I-93, follow Route 104 to Meredith, then Route 25 to Moultonboro, then take Route 109 to Center Sandwich village and the inn.

ACCOMMODATIONS: B & B $28 - $40
                  Dinner $ 5 - $10

Staffords-in-the-Field

Route 113

CHOCORUA, NEW HAMPSHIRE 03817

Telephone: 603-323-7766

Innkeepers: Fred and Ramona Stafford

Ramona still wonders why they bought the ramshackle old house some fifteen years ago, but lots of hard work and imagination have created a real New Hampshire *inn*stitution. During the summer the inn offers square dancing in the old barn, swimming in a natural pool in the Chocorua River, and a trail to the shores of beautiful Chocorua Lake. Cross-country skiing predominates in winter with many miles of trails, and touring skis are provided at no charge for the novice.

And in all seasons there is Ramona's cooking. Guests are seated in specific places in the large dining room, and Fred sits down to enjoy the meal with them. The one-entrée meals are "on the gourmet side," as Ramona says, with a variety of international and American dishes.

A typical meal may begin with fried mushrooms and pumpkin or peanut soup followed by salad with homemade dressing. Then would come garlic lemon potatoes, French peas or candied carrots, and pork tenderloin with prunes, leg of lamb, or sole Florentine. Breakfast, which includes freshly squeezed orange juice in season, is equally varied and might include something called Mexican Surprise.

The inn has twelve rooms in the main building, half of which have private baths. Four cottages, two used year-round, have living rooms, one to two bedrooms, and either a fireplace or a woodstove. Almost all of the beds are old, some brass and some four-posters, and most are doubles. Braided rugs and old dressers accent the old-fashioned appearance of the guest rooms.

The two sitting rooms have fireplaces and plenty of books and magazines. The inn's spacious grounds encourage outdoor activities in all seasons.

Open Memorial Day through October, December 26 through March. No charge cards, children over eight during the summer and holiday weeks only, liquor license. At Chocorua Village on Route 16, turn west and follow Route 113 for a short way. Watch for the small inn sign and a dirt road on the right.

ACCOMMODATIONS: *MAP* $84 - $95

Darby Field Inn
Bald Hill Road
CONWAY, NEW HAMPSHIRE 03818

Telephone: 603-447-2181

Innkeepers: Marc and Marily Donaldson

Darby Field was New Hampshire's first known mountaineer, being the first white man to climb Mt. Washington in the year 1642. Old Darby would feel right at home here for the view of Mt. Washington and other peaks are spectacular from the dining room and many of the guest rooms. With a thousand-foot elevation and somewhat isolated on a side road off the Kancamagus highway, this inn gives you the feeling of being at your own mountaintop retreat.

Marc has a restaurant background and has worked for Vermont inns. With his wife Marily, who is Spanish by way of Venezuela, Marc decided to run his own business. The dining room with the view is set up for elegant candlelight dining, with a menu that features various continental veal and chicken dishes — especially chicken Marquis — a breast of chicken sautéed with garlic, mushrooms, tomatoes, scallion, white wine and lemon juice, and chicken stock. With rainbow trout for an appetizer and homemade strawberry cheesecake or White Mountain maple chiffon pie for dessert, the dinner guest may adjourn to a spot before the huge fieldstone fireplace feeling amply rewarded. Fish of the day, scallops, and vegetable quiches are other menu choices.

Adjacent to the living room, which also has game tables and lots of books, is a small tavern with comfortable chairs and a woodstove.

Nine of the inn's eleven rooms have private baths, and our favorite is a large room with a queen-size bed with matching ornate dresser. Mountain lovers may request one of the rooms with the wide view across the valley.

There is a pool, and summer hiking trails become a large network of winter cross-country ski trails. Conway village is only 1½ miles away, and there are extensive hiking trails leading from the Kancamagus highway.

Open all year except in April and November through early December. (Open for Thanksgiving weekend, however.) Charge cards, children, liquor license. From Route 16, south of Conway village, turn left on Bald Hill Road for a mile or so, then right on a dirt road for another mile.

ACCOMMODATIONS: *MAP* $72 - $110

Palmer House Inn

Route 153

EATON CENTER, NEW HAMPSHIRE 03832

Telephone: 603-447-2120

Innkeepers: Frank and Mary Gospodarek

Nathaniel Palmer built this large house in 1884. Not long after, he began taking in boarders. The building was once a private school, but for the past five years it has been owned by the Gospodareks, who have restored and furnished it with Victorian antiques and other country pieces.

There are four double rooms sharing two baths, plus large family rooms and a bunk room, either suitable for large groups or big families. The Gardenia room with its antique bed is especially attractive.

A large common room for guests has a fireplace

and piano. Adjacent is the TV den with an old pump organ and lots of books. The pine-paneled dining room is open to the public by reservation. Both innkeepers cook and the one-entrée meals reflect their travels during the time Frank was in the State Department. Mary describes the menu as country French, but entrées vary from roast pork with baked apples and turkey with oyster/pecan stuffing to such north Italian specialties as chicken Bibioni. Inn smoked trout, turkey, and Cornish game hens are occasionally offered.

Fresh vegetables come from the inn's garden and for breakfast their own maple syrup and wild blueberries are featured. Soups and desserts are homemade.

There is swimming and sailing on Crystal Lake, and good fishing, too. Just down the road is the King Pine Ski area and Cranmore Mountain is about ten miles north. Nearby are miles of great hiking trails. For those less inclined to exercise, relax with a good book on the second floor balcony.

Open all year. No charge cards or liquor license, BYOB, children and well-behaved pets welcome. From Route 16 at Conway, follow Route 153 south six miles to Eaton Center.

ACCOMMODATIONS: *MAP* $64   Discounts for three days or longer.

Rock House Mountain Farm

EATON CENTER, NEW HAMPSHIRE 03832

Telephone: 603-447-2880

Innkeepers: The Edge family — John, Libby, Johnny, and Bill and Betsi Ela

This old farm has been welcoming summer guests since 1946. Children of early guests now come with their families, and they find the younger members of the Edge family have assumed most of the management of the inn.

Here is a vacation spot that harks back to the days when farmers took in a few summer boarders. Most guests are families who come for the week. Farm animals include cows, turkeys, dogs, cats, pigs, and geese, and they seem to enjoy the kids as much as the kids like them. Horses are out in the corral waiting for trail rides and just down the hill is picturesque Crystal Lake for swimming and boating at Rockhouse beach.

The one-entrée meals feature New England-style cooking with everything homemade. Roasts, turkey divan, beef Burgundy, and seafoods are popular here. The inn serves its own smoked ham, pickles, relishes and home-grown vegetables. Meals are family-style, with children gathering at their own table before the parents are served. For breakfast, choose from traditional New England favorites.

The recreation room has board games and ping pong; outside, you will find shuffleboard and other lawn games. Of course there are fields and trails to explore, and after a busy day of exercise, try the Finnish sauna.

The farm has seventeen rooms, four with private baths and the others sharing five hall baths. Three bunk rooms are popular with the young people. Furnishings are traditional and comfortable.

Two living rooms, one with fireplace, have lots of reading material, and one has a lovely antique Welsh dresser with English china.

Guests can sit and rock away the day on the farmhouse porch, but all are welcome to help get in the hay, haul some wood, or mend a fence or two.

Open mid-June through October. No charge cards, BYOB; children. Follow Route 16 toward the White Mountains and at Center Ossipee, turn east on Route 25, then Route 153 north to Eaton Center. At the sharp curve follow the dirt road up the hill to the farm.

ACCOMMODATIONS: *MAP* approximately $70

Fitzwilliam Inn

FITZWILLIAM, NEW HAMPSHIRE 03227

Telephone: 603-585-9000

Innkeepers: Charles and Barbara Wallace

Traditionally an inn served the traveling public as well as the local community. Since 1972, when the Wallaces acquired this old inn, they have attempted to make the place as important to the village today as it was when first opened in 1796. For example, the stagecoach doesn't stop here any more, but Vermont Transit Bus Lines does. Three northbound and three southbound busses daily connect the inn with Boston, Montreal, and several Vermont cities.

Since this tiny village, complete with old white

houses and churches spaced neatly around the village green, doesn't have a bank, Charlie arranged with a Keene bank, fourteen miles away, to allow the inn to take in deposits and make small withdrawals. It's easy, using the telephone and the bank's computer. Charlie is also a Justice of the Peace, so he can perform your marriage and then put you up for the honeymoon.

All of the above says nothing about the inn itself. It is as comfortable and charming as any old inn could be. The large, fireplaced living rooms are furnished in early American decor. The stenciling in one room is most attractive. And just down the hall is the rustic pub complete with a large fireplace, one of seven in the inn.

The large dining room has exposed beams and adjacent is a covered patio for summer dining next to the swimming pool. Three meals are served daily with the menu handwritten and presented on a bread board. Traditional food is featured including various steaks, chicken, trout, fish, and on weekends prime rib and leg of lamb. Barbara bakes the breads and makes the desserts.

The inn has twenty-two rooms and they use two nearby houses for overflow during busy times. The rooms are furnished with a combination of old and new pieces and they feature a wide range of double and twin beds. Some rooms combine well for family groups. About half have private baths.

Charlie is former manager of the Harvard and the Wellesley clubs, so he is an old hand at serving the public. But Barbara brings her own special talents to the inn: recently on the faculty of the New England Conservatory of Music, she is a professional musician and has many friends in the business. Each Sunday, January through March at 3:30 P.M., various combinations of musicians play a concert in the large living room. There is no charge, and both guests and the public are invited.

Open every day. Charge cards, liquor license. Pets

$3.00 extra. Just off Route 12, south of Keene in the village of Fitzwilliam.

ACCOMMODATIONS: *EP* $24 - $28
                                  Dinner $7.50 - $11

Inn at Crotched Mountain
Mountain Road
FRANCESTOWN, NEW HAMPSHIRE 03043

Telephone: 603-588-6840

Innkeepers: John and Rose Perry

"Country elegant" well describes this inn located high on the side of Crotched Mountain. Once the site of a large farm, the inn itself is housed in a 150-year-old building that was completely restored following a fire in the 1930s.

The living room, perhaps fifty feet long, has a fireplace at either end, comfortable high-backed chairs and sofas, and Oriental rugs. There's another fireplace in the small Winslow Tavern, and still another fireplace in the second, natural pine living room in a wing of the house.

Four of the fourteen rooms also have fireplaces,

making this place one of only a handful of inns that allow fires in guest rooms. Five of the rooms have private baths and all have easy chairs. There are both twin and double beds. Recalling the inconveniences of that great winter storm of '78 when most of New England was immobile for three days, we envy those few people who were marooned here at this fireplaced inn.

Both Perrys have professional hotel and restaurant training, although Rose does most of the cooking. King crab, lamb and pork chops, sirloin steak, and chicken teriyaki are among the dinner specialties. Many of the vegetables and herbs are grown on the premises. There is another fireplace in the comfortable dining room. Lunch is served in the summer only.

The inn's ten fireplaces consume about five cords of wood per year. John cuts most of the wood and "splits all of it."

Situated at an elevation of 1300 feet, the inn has fine cross-country skiing in the fields behind the house, and the Crotched Mountain ski area is just up the hill. The inn has two clay tennis courts and a swimming pool. Three golf courses are nearby.

Of course guests may just sit by the fires and occasionally gaze out of the windows to a forty-mile panoramic view across the valley of the Piscataquog River.

Open all year except for a few weeks in early November and after ski season ends. No charge cards, liquor license, pets accepted. From Peterborough take Route 202 north to Bennington, then follow Route 47 for 4½ miles. Turn right at signs for Crotched Mt. ski area and the inn is on the right.

ACCOMMODATIONS: *EP* $30 - $40
                  Dinner $7 - $12

The Horse and Hound Inn
Wells Road
FRANCONIA, NEW HAMPSHIRE 03580

Telephone: 603-823-5501

Innkeepers: Bob and Sybil Carey

This old building has been an inn since 1945, but the Careys have completely renovated it during their five-year ownership. Bob used to work in Boston television but he frequently visited Franconia, and with a love for cooking, he and the family decided to move north and open an inn.

Dinner is served in two large dining rooms, both with fireplaces and tall candles. The menu changes regularly and the chef likes to offer new recipes. Duck, veal, sirloin, chicken, Cornish game hen, and always a vegetable platter are entrée items. Everything is prepared from fresh ingredients and the inn makes its own breads and desserts. Vegetables come from the large garden. There is an extensive wine list that is worth reading — if only to see Bob's comments about each variety. Sunday brunch is served on a covered patio adjacent to extensive flower gardens. In fact, plants are much in evidence throughout the inn, and guests will also find fresh fruit in their rooms.

Classical music from Bob's extensive library is played during dinner and often Bob provides live music on the inn's piano located in the living room.

There are seven guest rooms, all with private baths. The rooms vary in size, but each is individually and brightly decorated with many old furnishings, each refinished by the Careys.

Franconia is surrounded by mountains, and trails for hiking and for cross-country and downhill skiing are near the inn, some within walking distance.

Open Memorial Day through October, December 26 to end of skiing. No charge cards, liquor license. Children discouraged. From Route 3 at the top of Franconia Notch, turn left and go past Mittersill, down the long hill and turn left on Wells road to the inn.

ACCOMMODATIONS: *EP* $40 - $55
        Dinner $8 - $16

Lovett's by Lafayette Brook
Routes 18 and 141
FRANCONIA, NEW HAMPSHIRE 03580

Telephone: 603-823-7761

Innkeepers: Mary Helen and Charles Lovett, Jr.

Just discuss Franconia with any old-timer and chances are he will first mention skiing and then Lovett's, for the two have been nearly a team since Cannon Mountain opened in the early 1930s. Actually, the inn began as a private home in 1784. That original owner was a surveyor who got the first road through Franconia Notch and he began taking in travelers soon thereafter. The Lovetts have been here since 1929, when they opened for summers, then added the winter season in 1932.

Charlie, who still does some of the cooking, shows

no sign of slowing down. In fact, he has even taken up cross-country skiing to supplement his longtime interest in downhill.

The inn has seven rooms, two with private baths and all with antique beds and sofas. Additional small cottages have two bedrooms each and nine of these rooms have fireplaces. The cottages are arranged with large windows offering views of Cannon Mountain.

The dining room, as befits an old house, has exposed beams and unusual hand-painted flowered wallpaper. There are several woodstoves, including one rare old wedding ring stove. The menu changes daily. It is quite varied because most guests stay for several days and many have been repeat customers for years. Charlie usually seats the guests to insure that everyone gets acquainted.

Chicken in brandy with herbs and cream, curried lamb, veal Marengo, broiled scrod, and ham steak are a few of the entrées. The desserts run the gamut from familiar hot Indian pudding with ice cream to mysteries called "Alaskan frostbite" and "acupuncture."

Breakfast features three kinds of shirred eggs, porridge, creamed finnan haddie, and even butternut and parsnip pancakes. Most of the vegetables come from the inn's own garden. The dining room is open to the public by reservation.

There is a comfortable sitting room with games and fireplace, and a small bar. The small lounge has an unusual marble bar, and there is also a porch-room.

You can swim in the inn's outdoor pool or the cold mountain brook nearby. Two trout ponds and the region's many brooks provide plenty of fishing. Golf, skiing, and mountain climbing are only minutes away. Lovett's package plans are especially popular with the winter skiing guests.

Open June to late October, December 26 through March. Credit cards, liquor license. From exit 37 on I-93, follow Route 18 south to the inn.

ACCOMMODATIONS: *MAP* $60 - $82

The Bernerhof Inn and Restaurant

Box 381   Route 302
GLEN, NEW HAMPSHIRE 03838

Telephone: 603-383-4414

Innkeepers: Ted and Sharon Wroblewski

The Bernerhof is another traditional North Country inn landmark that has made a comeback under the ownership of this friendly young couple.

Originally built as an inn in the 1890s, the place had more recently been operated just as a restaurant by Claire and Charlie Zumstein, a Swiss couple who created an old world atmosphere that the new owners have chosen to continue.

Ted and Sharon bought the inn while living in New York City where he was working for Dunkin Donuts.

Although Ted had worked for a hotel while in college, this was a new experience for him and Sharon.

After three years of renovations, they are beginning to feel comfortable with the old building, which has eight rooms with shared baths plus a sauna.

It is the restaurant that gets most of the attention here, and deservedly so. Ted is the chef, and he has continued many of Charlie's specialties plus a few new ones of his own. Six veal dishes are featured, including weiner schnitzel and Hungarian goulash. Both cheese and beef fondue are offered as well as beef Wellington, frogs' legs, bratwurst, and chateaubriand for two. For an appetizer try delices de gruyere (a smooth blend of Swiss cheeses, breaded and sautéed with tomato sauce), or Caesar salad for two.

For dessert, they offer chocolate fondue and cherries jubilee!

Among recent renovations is the Zumstein room, with rich oak paneling, a fireplace, brick arches, and a bar rescued from the old Crawford house. This is a comfortable spot for after dinner cocktails or dessert. And if you enjoyed a wine from the extensive list offered, they can sell many of the varieties offered to diners, for this is the only inn in New Hampshire that has a separate wine license.

Canoeing and swimming on the Saco River are only a short walk from the inn, and hikers can trek straight to Mt. Washington without crossing a road from the inn's back door. Ted has a liquid surprise for hikers and canoers; ask about it. Winter guests enjoy the sauna after exercising at nearby Attitash Ski area.

During dinner, the phantom pianist plays. The inn has a piano chorder, a computerized version of the old player piano, and some guests even dance or sing along to the music.

The season is from mid-December to mid-April; Memorial Day through October. Charge cards, liquor license, children. Located on Route 302 just above the intersection of Route 16.

ACCOMMODATIONS: *B & B* $40
                                MAP $60

The Back Side Inn
Rand Pond Road, RFD 2, Box 541
GOSHEN, NEW HAMPSHIRE 03773

Telephone: 603-863-5161

Innkeepers: Judi and John McMurray

This newly opened inn is on the back side of one of New Hampshire's finest state parks, Mount Sunapee. With skiing in winter and lake swimming in summer, there's plenty to keep the visitor busy.

Actually this 200-year-old plank house (notice the walls in the dining room) has been an inn several times in the past, but when the McMurrays moved up from Boston to set up innkeeping, the house had not been lived in for two years. "We never thought that we would have to do all that we did do," Judi says, but after eight months of work, the inn was ready to go.

Eight nicely furnished and decorated rooms share two baths, and there are rooms with both twin and double beds. The large living room has a reconstructed stone fireplace and big, soft sofas.

The dining room has several large old tables for family-style seating. Judi is the main cook, and breakfast includes blueberry pancakes, apple strudel, various eggs, sausage, and French toast. Dinner is served on weekends only and Sunday brunch is offered in the summer season, when diners may eat on the large glassed-in porch.

Two entrées are offered for dinner, usually gourmet items such as veal Marsala or chicken Kiev. The winter menu offers somewhat hardier fare. Dinner is open to the public by advance reservation, and there is one seating each evening. Summer guests should visit the crafts shop just across the street.

Open Memorial Day to mid-October; December 26 through March. Charge cards, BYOB. Just west of the Mount Sunapee traffic circle on Route 103, turn left on Rand Pond Road. The inn is several miles ahead on the right.

ACCOMMODATIONS: B & B $45
                 Dinner $8.50

John Hancock Inn
Main Street
HANCOCK, NEW HAMPSHIRE 03449

Telephone: 603-525-3318

Innkeepers: Glynn and Pat Wells

Built in 1879, this is the oldest continuously operated inn in New Hampshire, but we can't imagine that it ever could have been any friendlier than it is now.

The Wells family moved up here from New Jersey eight years ago. They left a small town, and they wanted to run an inn in a small town. Hancock is certainly small, but its main street is at least the loveliest in New England. Graceful churches and old houses with white wooden fences mark the village center and right in the middle of it all is the John Hancock Inn.

Traditionally, the country inn served the local people as well as the traveling public. This inn fits into the category exactly. Their dining room is open for three meals daily, and the menu is extremely diverse. Prime rib is offered daily along with veal scallopini, chicken almandine, and a variety of steaks. Roast duck and rainbow trout are also featured.

The steady stream of lunch customers is evidence of the local support given to the inn. Local organizations often meet here, too. There is likely to be a wedding reception in progress at any time. The inn is closed on Christmas Eve, when Glynn and Pat host an open house for town residents only. On Thanksgiving day each table gets a loaf of pumpkin bread, and for Mother's Day and Easter there are flowers for the ladies. Reservations are recommended for holiday dining.

There are ten rooms, all with private baths, but the most popular room has a canopy double bed with Rufus Porter murals on the walls. Porter, an itinerant painter of the mid-nineteenth century, lived nearby, but his work can be found in old houses throughout New England.

Most of the beds and furnishings are old, although several canopy beds are fine, locally made reproductions. The floors have handmade hooked and braided rugs.

The thirteenth in a continuous succession of owners, the Wells make everyone right at home. From the sitting areas in the upstairs halls to the main floor lounge with its carriage seats and tables made from old wooden bellows, the John Hancock Inn is quite comfortable. And it seems ready to provide service for the public for another two hundred years.

Open all year except Christmas Eve and Christmas day, and for a week in April and November. Liquor license, charge cards, pets. From Route 101 in Peter-

borough, follow Route 202 north and turn on Route 123 to Hancock and the inn.

ACCOMMODATIONS: *EP* $35
                  Dinner $7.25 to $11

Colby Hill Inn
The Oaks, Box 778
HENNIKER, NEW HAMPSHIRE 03242

Telephone: 603-428-3281

Innkeepers: The Glover Family

    Henniker is the only town on Earth so named. It is also the home of New England College and one of New England's most comfortable inns. Don and June Glover own the inn with son Don, Jr., who is manager and chef.

    Don calls his cooking "classical American," and it changes daily to take advantage of the season's freshest ingredients. The Glovers have a large garden, but they also buy from neighbors and local farmers' markets. Fresh fish is delivered daily from Gloucester fishing boats via a local market. Chicken, fish, shrimp, and veal dishes appear in many variations according to the chef's whim.

We enjoyed beef stroganoff and veal Marsala, each served with appetizer, large salads, fresh baked bread and rolls, and dessert (Indian pudding and English lemon curd). The wine list is extensive and mixed drinks are available from the small tavern just off the dining room. The dining room is closed on Monday nights, but otherwise is open to the public.

The inn's ten rooms, three with double beds and the rest with twins, are large and comfortable. Eight rooms have private baths. The living room and the television room are filled with comfortable chairs and the Glovers subscribe to more interesting magazines than do most libraries.

For those with patience, we recommend the continuous jigsaw puzzles or the most unusual checkerboard we have ever seen. Summer visitors can use the swimming pool. Nearby streams are convenient for canoeing, country roads for biking. Alpine and Nordic skiing and tennis courts are close by.

Colby Hill Inn was a working farm until 1959 when it was restored and converted to an inn. Five acres of fields and old barns remain. You are welcome to wander the fields behind the inn or investigate the old farm barn.

Winter guests, especially those from the city, have a real treat. Breakfast is served in a room with large west-facing windows. Just a few feet outside are several bird feeders. During our short visit we counted seven species of birds, and we suspect that many others are regular visitors depending on the season.

Open all year. Charge cards, liquor license, children over 6. Follow Route 9 from I-89 to Henniker and turn south at the village on Western Avenue for ½ mile to the inn.

ACCOMMODATIONS: EP $35 - $48
Dinner $8 - $14

Holiday Inn
Route 16A
INTERVALE, NEW HAMPSHIRE 03845

Telephone: 603-356-9772

Innkeepers: Bob and Lois Gregory

This Holiday Inn has been serving the traveler since 1890, and we suspect that the relaxed atmosphere created by the Gregorys during their six years here will please you more than anything available at the more famous motels with the same name.

The thirteen rooms, including three two-room suites, have private baths and are attractively furnished in the traditional style of a country inn. A small stone cottage originally built for a law office has two rooms.

Breakfast and dinner are served daily with two entrées offered most evenings. Pork chops, stews, ham, chicken, fish, and roasts are menu features with homemade rolls and desserts to round out the meal. Roast beef is served on Saturday night.

Lois cooks the breakfasts and some of the dinners, but usually she and Bob are in the dining room chatting with guests, giving them suggestions for activities and places to see in the area. Lois's doll collection and a large piano are living room accents, and there is also a TV room.

The inn's fifty acres include a small skating pond, swimming pool and twelve miles of cross-country trails. One mile of the trail is lighted and night tours are offered in connection with the New England Inn right next door.

A babbling brook flows beside the ski trails, and in summer this is a neat place for a quiet walk after dinner.

Open July through foliage season; December 26 to the end of skiing. Charge cards, BYOB. Located on Route 16A, just above North Conway.

ACCOMMODATIONS: MAP $70
B & B $44 (Summer only)

The New England Inn
Route 16A
INTERVALE, NEW HAMPSHIRE

Telephone: 603-356-5541

Innkeepers: Linda and Joe Johnston

With a name like The New England Inn one would expect to find a rambling old building with a lodging tradition dating back to the 1830s. And that is exactly what you'll find here. Originally built in 1809, the house was a stop for early settlers and teamsters long before tourists came to these mountains. Since the 1830s, the place has been a traditional inn and with various additions and many outbuildings it offers a wide variety of accommodations.

Tradition is still strong here. The restaurant is named for Anna Martin, who ran the inn with her husband for forty years. While the Johnstons bought the place about three years ago, their love and enthusiasm for the traditional qualities of country inns can match that of even the oldest innkeepers.

Three sitting rooms (two with fireplaces) and plenty of books welcome guests and give everyone a comfortable place to meet. Just off the large fireplaced dining room is the Intervale Tavern, which features low-keyed jazz and folk music nightly during holiday weeks and on weekends.

The inn itself has eleven rooms with private baths and six rooms that share baths. The decor is traditional and the Johnstons are gradually replacing the existing beds with colonial reproduction beds — comfortable and attractive.

There are thirty other rooms in various outbuildings. The five village houses have two suites each with fireplaces, sitting room, and baths. Just across the street is the meetinghouse, a 19th-century building with white pillars in front. It has guest rooms, a large function room for conferences or conventions, and also houses the inn's own ski touring center. Wednesday night ski tours on a lighted course are a special treat.

In the kitchen everything is cooked from scratch and at least three items change daily on the menu. Entrées include hunter's stew, varied steak, veal, and seafood dishes, and chicken Elizabeth — a breast of chicken with lobster tamale and king crab in a puff pastry with hollandaise.

The inn's three tennis courts are praised by the pro players who warm up here before the matches at the summer Volvo tennis tourney. There are also a pool and lots of lawn games.

Ask effervescent Linda about the special summer nostalgia five-day package, and guess who plays Santa during the traditional Christmas holiday festivities?

Bed and breakfast from Memorial Day to late June, then MAP *through the third week of October. Closed at the end of ski season to Memorial Day. Charge cards, liquor license, dogs only in the cottages. From Route 16 above North Conway, follow Route 16A at Intervale to the inn.*

ACCOMMODATIONS: *MAP* $100 - $152

Tuckerman's Inn and Tavern
Route 16
INTERVALE, NEW HAMPSHIRE 03845

Telephone: 603-356-2752

Innkeepers: Marge and Hugh Osborn

Perhaps the most famous view of Mt. Washington is across the intervale just above North Conway. That view accents this circa 1785 building that has been an inn since 1795. High on the side of Mt. Washington is Tuckerman Ravine, the landmark for which the inn is named.

The Osborns have just renovated and redecorated the building. Among the old features remaining is the large kitchen fireplace that is now a focal point of the dining room — if you can ignore the view of the mountain through the large windows.

The menu features northern Italian specialities with seven veal dishes. The chef's antipasto can be ordered for two and either Greek or Spinach salad is available as an entrée or split between two diners for an appetizer. Veal Piccata, veal Casa Linga, chicken Cacciatore, sole Amaretto, and lemon chicken are among the entrées. Several fish and steak dishes round out the menu.

During the winter, dinner is served Wednesday through Monday, with brunch on weekends. Lunch and dinner are served daily in summer months.

Tuck's Tavern, a newly developed English-style pub, has a piano. Hugh often accompanies the night's entertainer on his own guitar.

The inn has ten rooms, four with private baths, and all carpeted. Furnishings are eclectic and most rooms with shared baths have in-room sinks.

Open mid-May through foliage season, and mid-December through skiing season. Liquor license, charge cards. Located on Route 16 above North Conway.

ACCOMMODATIONS: *EP* with continental breakfast
$36 - $40
Dinners $8 - $11

Christmas Farm Inn
Route 16B
JACKSON, NEW HAMPSHIRE 03846

Telephone: 603-383-4313

Innkeepers: Bill and Sydna Zeliff

This cozy inn gets its name from a young woman whose father gave it to her as a Christmas present. She ran the place for a while as a farm, but eventually sold it to a couple who added "inn" to its name and Christmas Farm Inn it has been ever since. The details of this interesting inn's history are printed on the back of the menu.

The Zeliff family has been here since 1976, and they have continued the Christmas tradition with a red and white motif in the dining room and at a special "Christmas in July" celebration when Santa arrives in a horse-drawn buggy.

The Christmas traditions of hospitality and warmth are reflected throughout the year. Guests are personally shown to their rooms when checking in. Each room has a clock radio, carpeting, and free newspapers in the morning.

Sydna is the hostess in the dining room, which is open to the public. The thirteen-item menu varies from chicken Kiev and veal Marsala to sirloin steak and sole marguery. Most evenings the chef carves an ice sculpture to accent the salad bar, the latter something not found in most inns. Breakfast is served to guests and lunch is available on weekends.

Adjacent to the dining room and the comfortable living room is a tiny lounge where entertainment is offered. A second bar is located in a recently renovated barn that also has a sauna, a large recreation room with fireplace, games (perfect for children), and four bedroom suites. During the off season, the barn facility is used for small conferences and conventions.

Most of the twenty-seven rooms have private baths. Twelve rooms traditionally decorated are located in the main inn, which dates from 1786. The red 1777 saltbox has nine more deluxe rooms.

Ski touring trails connect with the 125-km network of the Jackson ski touring center and it is possible to arrange an inn-to-inn tour.

Open all year. Charge cards, liquor license. From Route 16, enter Jackson village and follow Route 16B up the hill to the inn.

ACCOMMODATIONS: *MAP* $64 - $96

Dana Place Inn
30 Pinkham Notch Road
JACKSON, NEW HAMPSHIRE 03846

Telephone: 603-383-6822

Innkeepers: Betty and Mal Jennings

Walk just a few steps from the front door of this 1890s inn and you'll see Mt. Washington, the highest peak in the Northeast, seeming to rise from the backyard. Located just at the southern edge of Pinkham Notch and surrounded by the White Mountain National Forest, Dana Place is a mountain lover's paradise.

From the inn you can walk or cross-country ski down the Ellis River valley to other inns in Jackson. A shuttle bus service is available for cross-country skiers, and hiking trails connect with paths leading all over the White Mountains.

The inn has tennis courts, a swimming pool, or use

of the natural pool in the river. Of course, you can fish in the Ellis River or perhaps just sit in a hammock and watch the river flow by.

The inn offers fourteen rooms, several with private baths, all with in-room sinks and some with king-size beds. There's a cozy reading lounge for house guests away from the main restaurant area of the inn. The inn also has a condominium complex and various two- and three-bedroom housekeeping units for minimum three-night stays.

Although the inn is nearly a hundred years old, it has been remodeled extensively on the main floor and reflects a more contemporary atmosphere. Three dining rooms, all interconnected, have large windows overlooking the surrounding forest. The menu is continental and features fish, beef, lamb, veal, and chicken. Entrées include rack of lamb for two, vegetable brochette, chicken Gloria, shrimp Stroganoff, and shrimp Archduke (sautéed with brandy, parsley, and artichoke hearts and baked with Swiss cheese in a béchamel sauce).

Appetizers, desserts, and wines are equally tempting. The inn specializes in a variety of after-dinner coffees with liqueurs.

During weekends and holiday weeks, hearty skier's lunch and fondue are served in the Pinkham Notch pub, where live music is also offered on weekends.

The Jennings have lots of experience in the hospitality business, and in their seven years here they have continued the traditions of innkeeping which the Danas established almost a century ago.

Open mid-June through October; Christmas week to mid-March; at other times open on weekends with no dining offered. Located right on Route 16 just north of Jackson, south of Pinkham notch.

ACCOMMODATIONS: *B & B* $48 - $64
Dinner $8.50 - $13.50

Whitneys' Village Inn
Route 16B at Black Mountain
JACKSON, NEW HAMPSHIRE 03846

Telephone: 603-383-6886

Innkeeper: Darrell Trapp

For nearly as long as there has been skiing in Jackson, there has been Whitneys' Village Inn. Once owned by the Moody family who used to take in summer boarders, the place was purchased by the Whitneys in 1936. A rope tow had been built on Black Mountain in 1935, and a few years later Bill Whitney erected his famous shovel-handle tow. The Whitneys sold their inn and the ski area in 1969, and the present owners acquired the building in 1979.

So much for history. Darrell is an energetic young man with extensive travel background and experience working for airlines. With a solid contemporary outlook on hospitality, he nevertheless seeks to create traditional New England graciousness at the inn.

For many guests, the stay at Whitneys' begins with afternoon tea at 4 P.M. Here guests and staff get to know each other, including the innkeepers, chef, and other house employees. Two living rooms are comfortably furnished with sofas and plenty of books.

Dinner is served in the Garden Spot, a bright room with a fireplace and the chef's indoor herb garden, offering views across the ski slopes. The dining room menu has received a number of awards for the continental and New England specialties served. Entrées include pork and lamb chops, seafood casserole, veal Marsala, chicken with shallots and sour cream sauce, and filet spitzen Estahazy — beef with vegetables and noodles.

Just completed is a new lounge called The Greenery. It seats just twenty-seven people and features sliding glass doors that open to the patio where in summer guests can settle into one of the old New England rockers for watching the sunset after supper. In the basement is a recreation room with ping pong, television, and games.

For more boisterous entertainment, especially during ski season, the rustic Shovel Handle Pub in a restored barn offers a piano player and lots of electronic games for the children. Lunch is served here during the ski season.

The overnight accommodations vary from quaint rooms featuring handmade quilts in the inn itself to three cottages with fireplaces (perfect for family groups), and a chalet with apartment-type quarters. One cottage, Brookside, is reached by crossing a bridge over a small brook.

Across the street from the inn is a small pond for summer swimming and lighted winter skating. Completing the traditional picture in the summer is a flock of sheep that grazes on hillside ski slopes.

Of course Jackson is also famous for cross-country skiing, and several of the inns, including Whitneys', have joined for an inn-to-inn ski week. Ask about it.

Open all year except dining room closed from April to May 28, November 1 to December 15. Charge cards, liquor license, children, pets in outer buildings only. Follow Route 16 to Jackson, go through the village and take 16B to Black Mountain and Whitneys'.

ACCOMMODATIONS: *MAP* $76 - $90

Thorn Hill Lodge

Thorn Hill Road

JACKSON VILLAGE, NEW HAMPSHIRE 03846

Telephone: 603-383-4242

Innkeepers: Donald and Gail Hechtle

Thorn Hill Lodge was built as a private summer home in 1895, became a boardinghouse in the 1920s and was converted to an inn in 1955. Don and Gail acquired the inn in 1980, but their friendly ways make them seem like longtime innkeepers.

Although Thorn Hill has recently changed to a modified American plan (from European), the dining room is open to the public and prices are reasonable. The menu changes with the season, although lobster pie is offered regularly. Seven to eight entrées, with daily specials plus homemade breads, quiche, and desserts complete the menu. Box lunches can be prepared and a full breakfast is offered daily.

The inn itself has twelve rooms, with two-room suites and both private and shared bath arrangements. Rooms are freshly decorated with a variety of antiques. Many of the bedrooms have that great view of Mt. Washington.

Also available are three cottages and a chalet with a fireplace and seven bedrooms.

The inn has a small lounge mainly for guests and the large living room, with pine paneling and fireplace, has books and games. Summer guests use the inn's pool or the tennis courts just a few hundred yards down the hill in the village.

Cross-country skiing is Jackson's prime attraction and trails from this inn connect with many other inns in the area and a 125-km trail network.

Open mid-December through the end of skiing, mid-May through foliage season. Charge cards, liquor license. From Route 16, pass through the covered bridge and turn right, up the hill in Jackson village.

ACCOMMODATIONS: MAP $86 - $98
                 Dinner $5.50 - $11

Wildcat Inn and Tavern

JACKSON VILLAGE, NEW HAMPSHIRE 03846

Telephone: 603-383-4245

Innkeepers: Marty and Pam Sweeney

Built in 1917 as an inn, the Wildcat is right in the middle of the village across the street from the ski touring center and tennis courts.

This is not a family inn, Marty explains, because the rooms are not large and there are no facilities for children. Six of the eighteen rooms have private baths and all rooms are comfortably furnished with braided rugs and twins, doubles, and some bunk beds.

Marty and Pam met while taking courses at the University of New Hampshire school of hotel administration. Marty, who has a master's degree and much experience in the business, is the inn's chef.

The entrées are original and all are cooked to order. The menu changes with the season, but typical entrées are seafood casserole, Wildcat chicken (a variety of chicken Cordon Bleu with a mustard sauce), mixed grills with pork, lamb, and sausage, and chicken martini (chunks of breast meat with artichokes and mushrooms baked in butter, garlic, and white wine). There is also a quiche of the day, a vegetarian specialty, steak, and fish dishes. Several food magazines have featured Marty's recipes.

The luncheon menu is equally varied and interesting, especially the lobster Benedict. Pam makes the inn's breads and desserts and cooks the lunch. The Sweeneys have been innkeepers since 1978.

The dining rooms are open to the public, but there are two living rooms for house guests only. Next door is the tavern with bar, two fireplaces, plenty of easy chairs, and entertainment on weekends and nightly during holiday weeks.

Above the tavern is a game room and out back is a heated waxing shed for cross-country skiers. Ski trails begin across the street and behind the inn. The golf course is only a good tee shot away and riding stables are nearby. Ice skating and sleigh rides are also available.

Open Memorial Day through October, December through mid-April. Charge cards, liquor license, no children. From Route 16, enter Jackson via the covered bridge — the inn is on the right.

ACCOMMODATIONS: *EP* $34 - $42
                 Dinner $6 to $12

The Monadnock Inn

JAFFREY CENTER, NEW HAMPSHIRE 03454

Telephone: 603-532-7001

Innkeeper: Sally Roberts

Just up the hill from this inn is one of the loveliest churches in New England and nearby is the grave of novelist Willa Cather who summered in Jaffrey. The village itself is attractive enough to be the subject of a magnificent book of photographs.

The best reason to visit Jaffrey Center, though, is the Monadnock Inn. Built in 1830, the inn has been serving the traveler since the 1840s, but perhaps never with better food than today.

Sally Roberts gives her three cooks free reign in the kitchen. All soups, stocks, sauces, and breads are made from scratch at the inn and the cooks use plenty of fresh herbs, butter, and cream. The dinner menu includes poached salmon with caper butter sauce, sauté of pork tenderloin in mustard sauce, and various steaks, chicken, and fish entrées. Don't miss the chocolate mousse for dessert. Three meals are served daily, except no meals served on Mondays in the winter.

There are three dining rooms, although summer guests prefer their lunch served on the screened-in porch. The living room, large and filled with easy chairs and sofas, has a fireplace but no television because, Sally says, "TV discourages the guests from talking with each other."

There are fourteen rooms, eight with private baths. The rooms have lots of windows and several may be combined as family suites.

And when *Gourmet* magazine featured three Monadnock region inns in a recent issue, the Monadnock Inn was included. " 'Nuff said!"

Open all year. Liquor license, children, no pets. From Route 202 in Jaffrey, follow Route 124 to Jaffrey Center.

ACCOMMODATIONS: *EP* $35
                                 Dinner $8 - $12.25

Beal House Inn

Main Street
LITTLETON, NEW HAMPSHIRE 03561

Telephone: 603-444-2661

Innkeepers: The Clickenger Family

    Doug and Brenda Clickenger got the inn bug while living in Florida, and they traveled 10,000 miles in seven months looking at inns before deciding on Beal House. The structure was built in 1833. Mrs. Beal had run the inn for forty years before it was purchased by the Clickengers.

    In a gradual process (now near completion), the new owners have refurbished the entire building, furnishing the rooms with antiques. If the lovely canopied double bed you sleep in appeals to you, it and most of the other furnishings are for sale. A nice antiques shop also occupies one wing of the building.

Each of the fourteen rooms is different, with a variety of twin and double beds. Several rooms are interconnected and are great for families. Most of the rooms have a private bath.

Doug is the breakfast cook, and the menu includes eggs, breakfast meats, waffles and freshly baked popovers. Brenda and daughters Alison and Alisa (on the weekends and in summer), dressed in colonial clothes, serve breakfast. Once when Doug was away, Alisa, then fourteen, cooked breakfast for thirty people.

Although the inn is located on the main street, it is outside the business area and with four acres of back yard, there's plenty of room for guests to take a walk before breakfast. A stereopticon viewer, player piano, and plenty of books contribute to cozy evenings in the living room.

Ticking clocks, braided rugs, spool beds, and a roaring fire in the breakfast room fireplace are only part of the charm of this inn. The friendliness and the hospitality of the innkeepers will make your stay memorable.

Open all year. BYOB, charge cards, children welcome. From exit 42 on I-93, go to Main Street and turn left for the inn.

ACCOMMODATIONS: *EP* $20 - $40
Breakfast $3.75

Edencroft Manor

Route 135

LITTLETON, NEW HAMPSHIRE 03561

Telephone: 603-444-6776

Innkeepers: Bill and Laurie Walsh/Barry and Ellie Bliss

Edencroft has been an inn for a number of years, but it had been closed for two years when these enterprising couples reopened it a year ago.

The couples vacationed together for a number of years and had often joked about running an inn. One day the joke got serious, and here they are.

Bill, who has professional hotel and marketing experience, is the chef while Ellie makes the pastries and fresh bread. Laurie, whose paintings hang throughout, is bartender, and Barry, who is maître d'hôtel, is also the maintenance man. Two professional waiters serve dinner in the candlelit dining room. Dessert and coffees are often served by the fire in the living room.

The inn has six rooms (one with a fireplace), and four of the rooms have private baths. The highlight of this inn, however, is the restaurant, serving three meals daily except Mondays. The full menu features beef, fish, and the house specialties of veal and duck. Recorded classical music plays throughout the main floor of the inn.

The lounge has large windows with southern views to the mountains and ski areas. The inn has eleven acres of land and plenty of wildlife — including Snow White, the skunk.

Open all year except during mud season in April. Charge cards, liquor license. The inn is located on Route 135 just a short drive from Route 18 and the temporary end of I-93.

ACCOMMODATIONS: *EP* $25 - $30
　　　　　　　　　　Dinner $7 - $11

The Lyme Inn
Route 10
LYME, NEW HAMPSHIRE 03768

Telephone: 603-795-2222 or 4404
Innkeepers: Fred and Judy Siemons

Picture a small New England village green with a Civil War memorial, and surrounded by old houses and a white church with carriage sheds, and you will envision Lyme, New Hampshire. At the head of the green, a place it has occupied since 1809, stands the Lyme Inn.

Fred and Judy have been here for four years, and they accent the antiquity of the place with many old pieces in both the guest quarters and the dining and living rooms. Sconces with tiny lights illuminate the dining rooms, where Hitchcock chairs and tables, wide pine floors, exposed beams, old baskets, and other domestic antiques complete the Colonial atmosphere. Old tools are displayed in the rustic tavern and in the guest rooms, antiques range from the beds to the chests and chairs. Four-poster twin beds and a matching painted bed and bureau set are set off by the traditional wallpapers. There are fifteen guest rooms, ten with private baths.

The menu is both traditional and continental. Shrimp fried in beer batter, sautéed scallops, and Alaskan king crab are seafood specialties, with hunter-style veal, hasenpfeffer (rabbit stew with bacon, onions, mushrooms, and sour cream), and weiner schnitzel among other entrées. Veal Morengo and garden casserole for two are offered as a light supper. The full country breakfast has a variety of eggs, pancakes, breads, and meats.

In the sitting room is a television, but more appealing are the many books and magazines. If you get involved with a book and have to leave before completing it, you are invited to take the book along and send it back when finished. Nearby Hanover is a center of cultural activities in all seasons and the Siemons have plenty of suggestions for things to do in the area.

Open early May through Thanksgiving; mid-December to late April. Charge cards, liquor license, children 8 and over. Follow Route 10 north of Hanover to the village green of Lyme. The inn is on the right at the head of the green.

ACCOMMODATIONS: B & B $40 - $55
                  Dinner or light supper $6.25 - $12.75

The Ram in the Thicket
Off Route 101
MILFORD, NEW HAMPSHIRE 03055

Telephone: 603-654-6440

Innkeepers: Dr. Andrew and Priscilla Tempelman

The Victorian mansion of the Abbott family who owned the large textile mills in Wilton was purchased by the Tempelmans and opened as a restaurant in 1977. The guest rooms were ready for business in 1980.

Priscilla and Dr. Tempelman, who is the minister at the nearby New Boston church, moved here from the Midwest. They wanted to change their lifestyles and open a small inn in New England.

Priscilla is the chef, assisted by two cooks. While she doesn't classify her menu, it is apparent that the offerings are a bit unusual: cherry almond pork, African lamb curry, fettuccini Florentine, and steak Bercy have been featured along with various other fish and steak dishes. The luncheon is equally tempting, with items of Chinese, French, Scotch, and German origins. Priscilla changes the menu with the seasons to take advantage of fresh fish and produce. The dessert menu changes daily.

The dining rooms are named according to the decor: Delft and Pewter Room, Brass Room, and Ivory and Crystal Room. The New Hampshire lounge is filled with hanging plants.

The six guest rooms have a variety of old brass, iron, and canopy beds. Two have private baths, and all rooms have recently been finished.

Continental breakfast is available to guests by request.

Open all year, but no meals on Mondays. Charge cards, liquor license. Located off Route 101, west of Milford, adjacent to Wilton. Watch for sign.

ACCOMMODATONS: *EP* $15 - $30
　　　　　　　　　 Dinner: $8 - $11

Hide-Away Lodge

NEW LONDON, NEW HAMPSHIRE 03257

Telephone: 603-526-4861
Innkeepers: Lilli and Wolf Heinberg

These innkeepers have been in the business since they were children, and in their eighteen years here they have established a manner of hospitality and service that is decidedly of the old school. Little things like warming a cup with hot water before pouring tea or coffee take extra time, but they indicate the special care given to all by this charming couple.

The inn itself is lovely. The interior is all natural Oregon fir, a costly treatment even when the building was constructed as a summer home in 1930. The several small dining rooms are simple but nicely appointed, as are the eight guest rooms, each with private bath. A scattering of books and magazines and the stone fireplace in the living room contribute to the relaxed atmosphere.

Outside are flower gardens and spacious lawns. A small rowboat now serves as a planter with fresh herbs for the kitchen. Nearby is Little Lake Sunapee for swimming or boating, and there are miles of marked woodland trails for quiet ambles between breakfast and dinner.

Dinner guests are shown to the screened porch where drinks may be ordered and menu selections are made. Since everything is cooked to order, guests may notify the waitress when they are ready to eat. Within minutes, you are shown to the dining room and the appetizer is served.

Caesar salad is made at your table, and other appetizers include garlic bread with mushrooms in snail butter, or champagne peach with Mission figs. Homemade soups vary from Danish fruit soup to carrot vichyssoise with julienne of scallions. Duckling with peach sauce is a mainstay, but lamb skewers marinated with herbs, rainbow trout, fresh Kennebec salmon, beef tenderloin with bearnaise or bordelaise sauce, and sautéed frogs' legs creole are other tempting entrées. In the fall, fresh venison, pheasant, and rabbit are offered.

Wolf, who prepares your salad and oversees the dining room, will also pour the wine. He is a wine expert, and if you arrive before dinner by all means ask to see his tidy wine cellar. It is as neat and clean as the rest of the inn, and he'll be glad to assist you in selecting a proper bit of grape for your table.

Hide-Away's special dessert is crepes pralinee flamed in apricot liquor, but cheese strudel, pistachio parfait with ginger slices, and plum sherbet with tawny port are equally tempting. June guests can have a champagne cocktail with wild strawberries picked by Wolf and Lilli each day.

If you have room for breakfast, Wolf will bring a cart to your table with fruit, cereals, and juices, but if he suggests his own eggs Benedictine or any other specialty, try it.

Open mid-May through October. No charge cards, but children and well-behaved pets welcome. Take exit 12 off I-89 and head toward New London village. Where the road bears right at a blinking light, turn sharply left at the traffic island and drive two miles to Little Lake Sunapee and bear right where the main road turns left. Follow this road through the woods to the hidden-away lodge. They'll be happy to meet your bus in New London or your plane in Lebanon.

ACCOMMODATIONS: *MAP* $70

New London Inn

NEW LONDON, NEW HAMPSHIRE 03257

Telephone: 603-526-2791

Innkeepers: Clara and George Adame

New London village was on the stagecoach route between Concord and Hanover. After 1792, when this inn was built, it became a popular overnight stop for travelers. It remains that today. New London is the home of Colby-Sawyer College and the New London summer playhouse. Nearby are Lake Sunapee and several ski areas, so the inn is a busy place in most any season.

Three meals are served daily in the main dining room, with lunch and light dinners available in Nelson's Tavern, the inn's rustic, informal lounge.

The dinner menu is continental with a variety of veal,

fowl and fish entrées. Seafood Combination includes swordfish, scallops, crabmeat, and shrimp baked in herb butter. Veal Oskar, steak au poivres, Alaskan deviled crab, roast duck, and baked rainbow trout are other specialties. The wine list is varied and inexpensive. Everything is cooked individually to order, even the vegetables.

There are twenty-four guest rooms all with private baths. Furnishings are eclectic, with some antiques and some newer pieces, all comfortable. The rooms have two doors, one with louvers so that guests can regulate the air flow in warm weather. The inn has two sitting rooms, each with a fireplace, and there is a fine library of books and magazines.

Open all year. Charge cards, liquor license. Just off I-89 in New London village.

ACCOMMODATIONS: *EP* $25 - $35
Dinner $8.25 - $13

Pleasant Lake Inn

North Pleasant Street
NEW LONDON, NEW HAMPSHIRE 03257

Telephone: 603-526-6271

Innkeepers: Branin and Linda Jaggard, Jerry and Sue Jaggard

A portion of this rambling inn was built as a center-chimney Cape in 1770 by one of the town's first settlers. About a hundred years ago the old building was converted from a farmhouse and expanded to become the Red Gables summer hotel. With the Pleasant Lake beach and reservoir-quality water just across the country road, Red Gables became a most popular resort.

For the past four years, these two young couples have worked to continue that old innkeeping tradition. The renamed inn has twelve rooms, one with private bath and several others with in-room sinks. Bedrooms have antiques and older pieces accented by braided rugs. There are great views in all seasons across Pleasant Lake to the hills of central New Hampshire.

The inn has two dining rooms, and one is part of that old 1770 Cape. Here, massive exposed beams and wide pine floors are complemented by several antique chests and sideboards. The dining rooms are open to the public for both dinner and breakfast.

Chicken Pleasant Lake (breast of chicken with scallop and asparagus stuffing in a light Newburg sauce) is the house specialty. Other dishes include veal Marsala, coquille St. Jacques, baked sole, and prime rib on the weekends. Sunday brunch offering fancy egg dishes, omelets, and blintzes is served during summer and fall. The public dining room is closed on Tuesdays.

Breakfast and cocktails are served on the patio in warm weather, but the inn also has a large living room with a bar, piano, fireplace, and comfortable chairs and sofas.

Cross-country trails and a nine-mile hiking trail are nearby, and Pleasant Lake offers recreation year-round, from sailing to ice fishing. The inn offers a variety of package plans both winter and summer.

Open all year except for April and a week late in November. Charge cards, liquor license. To get there from New London village, turn between Kidder's garage and the market and follow North Pleasant Street down a long hill to the inn and lake.

ACCOMMODATIONS: *EP* $28 - $34
                  Dinner $8 - $10

Indian Shutters Inn
Route 12
NORTH CHARLESTOWN, NEW HAMPSHIRE 03603

Telephone: 603-826-4445

Innkeeper: Bud Elliot

One of the most popular restaurants in western New Hampshire, Indian Shutters now has four guest rooms and in the summer has a few cabins open to travelers.

This old building was first opened as a tavern in the 1790s and its name comes from the sliding, paneled wooden shutters in the first floor rooms. There are three smaller dining rooms in the main house and a larger one in the remodeled stable. Here old beams are accented with a huge stained glass window that has been converted into a chandelier. Old chairs and linen tablecloths complete the decor.

Luncheon and dinner menus are diverse and range from pot roast and chicken pie to seafood Newburg and chicken Cordon Bleu. Everything is homemade here including the pies, breads, and the popular sticky buns.

The guest rooms are all large, with wide pine boards, wainscoting, and fireplaces, although the latter are not used. Three rooms have double beds, and there are two shared baths.

Bud Elliot is especially proud of the local produce that is featured in season. Strawberries, apples, corn, potatoes, huge raspberries, and other vegetables are all grown on local farms.

Open all year except Christmas Eve. Charge cards, liquor license. Just off Route 12 north of the village of Charlestown.

ACCOMMODATIONS: EP $28
                  Dinner $7 - $13

Cranmore Mountain Lodge
Kearsarge Road
NORTH CONWAY, NEW HAMPSHIRE 03860

Telephone: 603-356-2044

Innkeepers: Dawn and Bob Brauel

Tucked away from the hustle of downtown North Conway and with views of its namesake mountain, this inn has made a comeback in the three years this young couple has owned it. Open to guests since the late 1890s, the inn has been completely renovated, freshly papered and painted, and outfitted with a number of facilities for active vacationers.

A new swimming pool, "the best hard surface tennis court in the Valley," plus an outdoor Jacuzzi bath, fishing pond (flyfishing, no keepers), and a trout stream will keep summer visitors busy. Winter guests may rent downhill equipment from the inn's shop, skate on the lighted fish pond, or scoot down the toboggan hill. Cross-country trails begin on the property.

The main inn building has eleven rooms with shared baths featuring various combinations of twins, double, and bunk beds. Most of the rooms also have sinks. The converted barn has four modernized rooms with private baths and two double beds, a recreation room plus a four-room dorm that sleeps forty and is popular in all seasons with groups. Chaperones are required for young people's groups.

One-entrée dinners are served nightly in the winter and by request for groups in other seasons. Homemade soups are the appetizers for such main dishes as roast beef, baked chicken, ham, lasagna, and other home-style favorites. The full breakfasts feature eggs, muffins, and pancakes.

There are two living rooms, and one, with pine paneling and fireplace, has a special bit of history attached to it. Ask Dawn or Bob about it.

Open all year. Charge cards. From Route 16 above North Conway, turn east on Hurricane Mountain Road, turn right on Kearsarge Road. The inn is on the left.

ACCOMMODATIONS: *MAP* (winter only) $51 - $64
EP (summer, dinner by request) $25 - $43
Breakfast $2.75

Stonehurst Manor
off Route 16
NORTH CONWAY, NEW HAMPSHIRE 03860

Telephone: 603-356-3114

Innkeeper: Peter Rattay

Wealthy Victorians knew how to build impressive summer homes, and this inn is one of them. Constructed in 1876 by the Bigelow carpet family, the building has a stone first story and a rich oak interior, leaded windows, ornate mantlepieces, and a huge front door.

The inn was completely refurbished and redecorated two years ago when Peter became innkeeper. Most of the public rooms and the bedrooms now have been furnished to match the architecture. Two dining rooms, one with large white wicker chairs, the other with natural wood wicker, are elegant. The wicker motif extends to many of the bedrooms as well.

There are twenty-seven rooms, with seventeen in the main section of the inn, twelve with private baths. Ten rooms with private baths are in the annex. Some of the rooms have balconies, all have television and some have air conditioning. Many of the rooms are huge, and the decor varies throughout the inn.

The former study is now the lounge, and here an ornate fireplace and exquisite leaded windows are the accents. A piano chorder, sort of a computerized player-piano, provides music for dining. A door leads to the patio where Sunday brunch is served in warmer months. Drinks are also served at the outdoor, wooden-sided pool.

Although this estate once covered six hundred acres, the inn now has thirty acres, but its location, well removed from the main highway with tall pines and broad lawns, is still impressive. The pool, tennis courts and 28-km of cross-country trails are available for energetic guests.

Open all year. Charge cards, liquor license, well behaved pets welcome. Located just off Route 16 above North Conway village.

ACCOMMODATIONS: *EP* $28 - $82 (suite)
                  MAP add $18.95 per person

Follansbee Inn

NORTH SUTTON, NEW HAMPSHIRE 03260

Telephone: 603-927-4221

Innkeepers: Larry and Joan Wadman

This building was the annex to the original inn that was built here in 1897. This inn was just a farmhouse, but it has been expanded over the years and became the main inn in the early 1960s. The Wadmans have completely refurbished the place with new carpeting and wallpaper. Several new bathrooms have been installed. The inn has twenty-three rooms, eleven with private baths. The rooms have both new and older double and twin beds. Daughter Wendy, who works at the inn, makes handicrafts for sale.

The dining is continental and prepared by a professional chef. Veal vermouth, chicken Cordon Bleu, beef tenderloin medallions, baked stuffed trout, and swordfish Dijonaise are only a few entrées offered. Everything is cooked to order and the chef makes the soups, breads, salad dressings and desserts.

There are two dining rooms, each furnished with comfortable chairs, and the guests are encouraged to enjoy a leisurely candlelit dinner. The inn has a cozy lounge with a fireplace. The dining room is closed on Monday.

Kezar Lake, one of New Hampshire's prettiest, is just across the country lane from the inn, and there is a golf course nearby. Winter guests enjoy several ski areas, and in the summer the New London Playhouse is only a short drive away.

Open all year except for a few weeks in April and November. Charge cards, liquor license, children. From exit 10 on I-89, follow the signs south to North Sutton and turn right on Route 114 to the village and the inn.

ACCOMMODATIONS: *EP* $21 - $32
 MAP minimum of three day stay $55 - $64
 Dinner $6 to $14.50

The Inn at Christian Shore
Maplewood Avenue
PORTSMOUTH, NEW HAMPSHIRE 03801

Telephone: 603-431-6770

Innkeepers: Charles Litchfield, Tom Towey, and Louis Sochia

These three men have restored six houses, but this is their first experience in running an inn. It is obviously a calling to which they are well suited. They bought this old house, restored and furnished it with a variety of antiques, and opened their doors to the public about two years ago.

Food is an essential part of any inn, and here they serve breakfast and occasionally Sunday brunch.

Breakfast is a five course meal served from 7 until 9:30 A.M. Juice or fresh fruit, sometimes with sherbet, is the first course followed by home-baked sweet breads, steak or pork tenderloin, omelet or other eggs, a vegetable, home fries, and toast plus coffee or tea. The menu changes daily so that guests staying more than one night will have something new each morning.

The innkeepers used to be in the antiques business, so they have furnished the inn with a variety of fine old pieces. There are five rooms, including two with double beds and private baths. Two baths serve the other three rooms. Guests are welcome to play the organ in the living room.

Just behind the inn is the Jackson house, one of Portsmouth's oldest dwellings and open to the public in the summer. Within a ten-minute walk are downtown Portsmouth and other historic houses as well as Portsmouth's diverse, well-known restaurants. By advance notice, the innkeepers are happy to meet travelers at Portsmouth's bus terminals.

Open all year. Charge cards. From Portsmouth's Market Square, travel south through two lights, turn right on Maplewood, go through two more lights. The inn is on the right at the base of a small hill. From I-95, take exit 6 and turn right on Woodbury Avenue. Opposite the Holiday Inn, turn left on Dennett Street and follow to the end. The inn is right across the street.

ACCOMMODATIONS: B & B $35 - $40

Martin Hill Inn
404 Islington Street
PORTSMOUTH, NEW HAMPSHIRE 03801

Telephone: 603-436-2287

Innkeeper: Alexandra Gebow

Elegant is not a term that usually describes a bed and breakfast inn, but it fits Martin Hill nicely. Situated just ten minutes' walk from downtown Portsmouth with its diverse restaurants and the Strawbery Banke restoration, Martin Hill Inn has six lovely rooms each with private bath and air conditioning.

All of the rooms are different although the master bedroom with its canopy bed and rich wallpaper is especially attractive. This inn is actually two buildings. The main house, circa 1820, has three bedrooms, the common room, and kitchen, while the 1850 annex just next door has three other rooms. There is off-street parking and a large backyard with flowers and two brick patios.

The four-course breakfast varies daily, but it usually includes fresh fruit, marinated pork chops or steak, scrambled eggs with thyme, German apple pancakes, or hash with dropped eggs, freshly baked scones or bread and tea or coffee.

Europeans are especially attracted to bed and breakfast inns, and one morning last summer the dining room had guests from four foreign countries. Innkeeper Gebow, who is German, speaks four languages, so everyone felt right at home. And a feeling of being right at home is exactly the atmosphere one finds at Martin Hill.

Open all year. Charge cards. From I-95, take the Woodbury Avenue exit east and turn left at Islington Street lights. The inn is a couple of blocks ahead on the right.

ACCOMMODATIONS: *B & B* $25 - $35

Philbrook Farm Inn

North Road
SHELBURNE, NEW HAMPSHIRE 03581

Telephone: 603-466-3831

Innkeepers: Nancy Philbrook and Connie Philbrook Leger

Sisters Nancy and Connie are the fourth generation of Philbrooks to operate this inn that began in 1861 by their great-grandfather, Harvey. His portrait still hangs by the fireplace in one of the three living rooms, and we suspect that he would approve of the simplicity and friendliness that marks the inn's atmosphere today.

Connie, Shelburne's town clerk, and Nancy, supervisor of the checklist, have been at the inn since the 1940s and assumed active management when their father Lawrence died in the mid-'70s. Connie's son Larry, the fifth generation, was the waiter the night we were at the inn.

If the foregoing sounds like a history lesson, it was meant to be. This inn is a White Mountain history lesson in disguise. The walls are lined with old prints, lithographs, and maps of the White Mountains. In the large living room is a rare antique stereopticon viewer with pictures of the area and the inn when Harvey was alive. One closet holds old books of White Mountain history and volumes written by former guests. Another has a collection of homemade wooden jigsaw puzzles created by Augustus Philbrook — he of the second generation. Augustus also made many pieces of furniture in the inn, and even the models he built prior to making the full-size pieces are on display here.

The inn itself has nineteen rooms, six with private baths, and the remainder have one bath for each two rooms. As might be expected in an inn operated by the same family for over 120 years, the furnishings in the rooms are mostly old pieces, and the decor is traditional New England. Many of the paintings were done by guests.

Each bedroom also has a curtain in the doorway covering the opening. During warm summer nights or cold winter nights, the doors can be left open to control the temperature yet maintain privacy.

The inn also has one small and five large cottages that are available by the week just in the warmer months as they are heated only by fireplaces. The cottages have up to four bedrooms, and pets are allowed. No pets are allowed in the main inn.

Meals are served daily, and almost everything is cooked on a big old black woodstove, even in summer. One kitchen wall has the largest collection of cast iron fry pans we have ever seen.

Lunch and dinner feature one entrée only, with

roasts a specialty and traditional New England home-style cooking featured. Saturday night's dinner is always baked beans and Sunday noon it's roast chicken. Sunday breakfast offers fish balls and corn bread, plus the eggs and cereals served daily for breakfast. Box lunches are put up for guests who will be away for the day. The spacious dining room has windows to the south. From the farm gardens come fresh vegetables, and all the jams, jellies, and pickles are homemade.

During the winter the inn caters to skiers, but in the warmer months it is the perfect spot for families. The inn is on several hundred acres of land and offers many lawn games plus swimming in the brook on rocky slides. Hiking paths lead from the inn to the Appalachian Trail, which runs from Maine to Georgia.

Open from May through October, and December 26th through March. No charge cards, BYOB. Located off Route 2, east of Gorham, on North Road.

ACCOMMODATIONS: MAP $55 - $63, special rates for children 12 and under. Weekly rate includes lunch $200 - $225 per person.

Snowvillage Inn

Box 117

SNOWVILLE, NEW HAMPSHIRE 03849

Telephone: 603-447-2818

Innkeepers: Pat and Ginger Blymyer

For many people, the lure of Hollywood and hob-nobbing with movie stars would be the dream of a lifetime. For many years it was exciting for the Blymyers. Pat, a lighting expert, and Ginger, a hairdresser, have worked for years on major movies, and while they still return to the lights and glitter occasionally, they seem quite content with their country inn tucked away in a small village in the foothills of the White Mountains.

Snowvillage Lodge was built as an author's summer home in 1916, but it has been an inn since 1948. For the

Blymyers, who have been here for five years, the inn offered the chance to continue working with people, but in a country location, a place they could call home.

The lodge is high on a hillside and one can easily imagine the view from the porch of the sun setting on the slopes of Mt. Washington, New Hampshire's highest peak. For some guests, the panorama is so exciting that they spend an entire vacation right at the inn.

Snowvillage Inn has fourteen rooms, all with private baths, including eight rooms in the remodeled barn, where room doors open to the center of the barn which has been left as a common area for guests to sit and chat or read. All rooms are furnished with a variety of traditional and older pieces, with twin and double beds.

The one-entrée meals are served in the spacious dining room with its large windows and Oriental rugs. Veal picatta is the house specialty, but chicken curry with peaches, baked ham, stuffed pork chops, chicken Florentine and occasional vegetarian dishes are offered. A neighbor grows the inn's fresh vegetables and they make their own soups (blueberry), breads, and desserts (French silk pie and chocolate mousse).

Sunday breakfast is eggs Benedict with champagne, but each morning a surprise pancake is featured along with freshly baked muffins.

The living room is large with a fireplace, grand piano, and a great library with books covering about every possible subject. For those needing more exercise, the inn has a tennis court, swimming and boating on nearby Crystal Lake, and a cross-country ski center and sauna for winter guests.

And we can't forget Gracie, the friendly Yorkshire pig. Now too large to have the run of the inn, she nevertheless welcomes every guest from her private lodgings, The Gracie Mansion.

Open all year. Charge cards, liquor license, children and well-behaved pets. From Route 16 at Center Ossipee, follow Route 25, then take Route 153 to Eaton. Just beyond Crystal Lake, turn right to Snowville, and watch for signs of the inn.

ACCOMMODATIONS: *MAP* $90

Pitcher Mountain Inn
Route 123
STODDARD CENTER, NEW HAMPSHIRE 03464

Telephone: 603-446-7000

Innkeepers: Bill and Dawn Matthews

Here the emphasis is on the dining room, and the inn's reputation for good food prepared by this young couple is well deserved. Dawn makes the breads and pastries and runs the dining rooms while Bill is the entrée chef.

Bill changes the menu occasionally so that he can utilize the fresh foods in season. They have their own vegetable and herb gardens, the latter with some forty varieties, and they drive nearly five hundred miles each week to pick up fresh fish and other ingredients.

Scallops Provençale, breast of chicken Normandie

and lamb brochette are some of the entrées, while the summer menu may include swordfish, lobsters, squid, and bluefish. Bill cooks with a liberal use of cognac and white wine and all the food shows his light touch.

Homemade soups, pâté, and other appetizers complement the main entrées. Our salad of romaine with an herb, oil, and vinegar dressing sprinkled with blue cheese was a pleasant change from most creamy cheese dressings. Summer salads include edible flowers.

There are two dining rooms, one suitable for private parties, and the other larger with a fireplace and lots of windows. The lounge occupies the front parlor of this 1830 Colonial, and the three guest rooms, which share a bath and are each small but comfortably furnished, are in the ell.

The wine list is a photo essay with pictures by Bill, and since he is also a musician there are often impromptu and scheduled musical entertainments.

Stoddard is just a village with lots of summer lakeside homes, but not too much to attract the tourist except for the Pitcher Mountain Inn. It is worth the visit. *Gourmet* magazine thought so, too, when the inn was featured in a recent issue.

Open April through foliage season, Thanksgiving, and after Christmas through February. Closed Monday and Tuesday. Sunday brunch is served, and lunch is available in summer and fall. Charge cards, liquor license. From Keene, follow Routes 10 or 9 north to Route 123 and Stoddard.

ACCOMMODATIONS: *EP* with Continental breakfast $30
Dinner $8.50 - $14

The Homestead
Route 117
SUGAR HILL, NEW HAMPSHIRE 03585

Telephone: 603-823-5564
Innkeeper: Esther Serafini

Many country inns work hard at being what The Homestead is naturally. All of the furnishings here are antiques, each one inherited from family members who settled Sugar Hill 200 years ago and who began this family inn in 1880. Esther, called Essie by friends and guests alike, can tell you a story about most any bed, rug, chest or wall hanging. And she's quite a story herself. She began working here at the age of ten, passing the relish tray, and sixty years later she is still here, helped out by grandchildren who are the seventh generation members of the town's first family.

Each of the inn's seventeen rooms is different. After all, you can't buy matching sets of antiques any more. The beds, whether twins or doubles, are antiques too. One was originally hauled up Sugar Hill in the late 1700s by Moses Aldrich, the first settler. Seven rooms have private baths and there is a seven-bedroom cottage and a one-bedroom chalet just across the street from the inn. It seems that any furnishing that isn't an antique has some special story attached to it, and Essie delights in talking with her guests about the family and the inn.

A large organ, a gift to Essie in 1980 on the inn's hundredth birthday, dominates one living room, and a huge hooked rug map of New Hampshire made by Essie hangs on the wall as the focal point of another. Books and magazines, new and old, are everywhere for guests' enjoyment.

All of this antiquing builds up a powerful appetite, and the inn is well-equipped to handle the problem. Everything is made from scratch and cooked according to the century-old family recipe collection.

New England style cooking it is, and good enough to have been featured in *Cuisine*, *Playboy*, and a host of other magazines and books. Baked sirloin Homestead-style, stuffed thick pork chops, boneless chicken fried in special butter with onion rings, turkey, and roast beef are among the one-entrée dinners. Both fish and meat dishes are offered on Friday nights.

Homemade soups, jellies, maple butter, breads, candied ginger parfait, strawberry rhubarb shortcake, peanut butter pie — the list is endless and ever-changing.

And after dinner in any season walk up the hill behind the inn to what has to be the best mountain view in all New England. The Franconia range, and behind it the Presidential range, seem to rise up near enough to touch.

When you have to leave the inn, Essie and the other guests will gather with old bells and ring you on your way.

Open May through October; Thanksgiving Day and weekend; Christmas through March. No charge cards, BYOB. Jackets required for gentlemen diners. On Route 17 midway between Franconia and Lisbon. From exit 38 on I-93, turn north in Franconia village, then turn left on Route 117 up the hill to The Homestead.

ACCOMMODATIONS: *MAP* $70 - $80

Sunset Hill House

SUGAR HILL, NEW HAMPSHIRE 03585

Telephone: 603-823-5522

Innkeepers: Betty Lou Carmichel and Douglas A. Reed

This inn seems like a return to innkeeping as it was known in the White Mountains a hundred years ago. Situated high on Sugar Hill with fabulous views of the Franconia Range and Cannon Mountain, this Sunset Hill house was part of the huge old Sugar Hill House that was taken down a few years ago.

Eddie, a bellhop from the old school, will help you with your bags, and depending on the season, the nine hole golf course, cross-country ski center, pool, or paddle tennis await your pleasure.

Three meals are served daily (full breakfast and

dinner on *MAP*) featuring a traditional New England-style menu with homemade soups and breads. Typical entrées are broiled Atlantic salmon, sautéed sirloin tips, lobster, veal Provençale and chicken Francaise. Breakfast features eggs, omelets, codfish cakes, and creamed chipped beef. Lunch is served beside the pool in summer.

There are three sitting rooms for house guests plus a full-service bar and lounge. The thirty-five guest rooms, all with private baths, have recently been wallpapered and painted by Betty Lou and Douglas, who ran the inn for four years before becoming the owners three years ago. They have extensive innkeeping experience and they enjoy maintaining the traditions of this old hostelry.

Holidays are always special here, with a cookout and fireworks on July Fourth and a visit from Santa and a church service on Christmas Eve. Winter events include sugar-on-snow parties and a cookout on weekends at the cross-country ski center. They even have a Work Bee weekend at Thanksgiving when guests help make Christmas decorations, haul wood, and clear ski trails. Guests help carve the turkey, and the inn offers a special rate for the four-day weekend.

And don't miss the clubhouse. Used for golfers and cross-country skiers, it was built in 1900 and at the time was considered the finest at any of the numerous White Mountain hotels.

Open all year. Charge cards, liquor license, children and pets. From exit 38 on I-93, turn right in Franconia village, then left on Route 117 to the top of Sugar Hill. Turn left by The Homestead and follow the ridge a few hundred yards to the inn.

ACCOMMODATIONS: *MAP* $85 - $95

Dexter's Inn

Box 100, Stagecoach Road
SUNAPEE, NEW HAMPSHIRE 03782

Telephone: 603-763-5571

Innkeepers: Frank and Shirley Simpson

High on a hill overlooking Lake Sunapee, Dexter's Inn is a 150-year-old house converted to comfortable accommodations for travelers, vacationers, and especially tennis players.

There are three tennis courts and a teaching pro. Sometimes there are informal tournaments and court time can be reserved for those special matches against fellow hard-serving guests. And after a hot day on the courts, relax in the large swimming pool or enjoy a cold drink on the terrace.

There are ten rooms in the main inn and seven more

in the annex, a remodeled barn just across the drive. The annex also has a recreation room with ping pong and other games. Guest rooms, all with private baths, are brightly wallpapered, carpeted, and have a mixture of antiques and other pieces. One room has grandmother's canopy bed and some larger rooms have king-size beds.

The dining room is in the main inn. Two entrées are offered nightly. Baked scallops in cheese and wine, London broil, veal Cordon Bleu, or sole almandine are among the varied entrées. Lunch is served on the patio in July and August, and the full country breakfast includes homemade marmalade. On request, breakfast is served in bed at additional charge.

The living room has a fireplace, grand piano, and lots of books. Drinks are served from the small cocktail lounge. The inn also has housekeeping units (rented by the week) in the woods about one-quarter of a mile from the inn.

Frank has recently decided to close the inn for part of the winter, but his cross-country trails are open for day skiers on weekends and are great hiking paths in summer. And if you want to come down from the inn's 1400-foot elevation, you'll find great swimming and boating on Lake Sunapee and several summer theaters nearby.

Open May through October. No charge cards. Liquor license, children, pets $3 a day in annex only. From exit 12 on I-89, follow Route 11 for eight miles past the village of Sunapee, then turn left at the inn sign up Winn Hill Road 1½ miles to the inn.

ACCOMMODATIONS: *MAP* $75 - $90, July, August and early October
EP available in June and September
B & B available in May and late October

Tamworth Inn

TAMWORTH, NEW HAMPSHIRE 03886

Telephone: 603-323-7721

Innkeepers: Larry and Kelly Hubbell

This is an old village inn serving local people as well as visitors in all seasons. Built in 1850, the inn is traditionally furnished with some antiques and New England wallpapers and paints.

This young couple has just taken over the inn and they are enthusiastically planning a few changes. Steak au poivre remains a popular menu item along with scallops Tamworth and veal Provençale. Onion soup is also a specialty. Three meals are served daily, except no lunch or dinner on Monday during the busy seasons. Brunch is served every Sunday. During slow periods, dinner is served Thursday through Sunday.

Ten of the inn's twenty-one rooms have private baths, and furnishings range from old four-posters to more modern pieces. Some rooms have original wall paintings dating back to 1850. There's fresh fruit in each room and an early morning call service with coffee served in your room.

One of the three common rooms is a TV den, while another has a fireplace, an old organ, and shelves of books. The inn has its own pub with full service bar and a woodstove to warm you after a day of downhill or cross-country skiing.

A swimming pool and other backyard activities are available including croquet, softball, badminton, and fishing. The inn is surrounded by country roads for bike riding. Across the street is the old white church and a pasture with horses. Covered bridges, beautiful Chocorua Lake, and miles of hiking trails are nearby.

During the summer, a perfect day includes dinner at the inn, then a short walk down the street to The Barnstormers, New Hampshire's oldest summer theater.

Open all year except late October to mid-November, March to mid-April. Charge cards, liquor license, children, no pets, but a kennel is nearby. From Route 16 at Chocorua, or Route 25 at Whittier, follow Route 113 to Tamworth village. At the crossroads, head west a short distance to the inn.

ACCOMMODATIONS: *EP* $30 - $40
Dinner $7.25 - $13.50
Mid-week *MAP* packages available

Birchwood Inn

Route 45

TEMPLE, NEW HAMPSHIRE 03084

Telephone: 603-878-3285

Innkeepers: Bill and Judy Wolfe

Birchwood Inn dates from 1775 although the existing brick building was probably constructed about 1800. It had been a private home for about fifteen years when the Wolfes acquired it and opened for business on July 5, 1980. For eight months before opening, they purchased and designated each piece of furniture for each room. More than sixty pieces were refinished by Bill and Judy.

By starting from scratch, the Wolfes have been able to decorate each room to a specific theme. Depending on other reservations, the guest can select from seven rooms devoted to the seashore, trains, library, old bottles, editorial, school, and music. The rooms have a variety of twin and double beds, and all rooms share baths.

Both Bill and Judy cook; she prepares the breads, relishes, and desserts. He does the entrées. Both breakfast and dinner are open to the public, and since this is the only eating place in town, many local people dine here.

Two entrées are served for dinner, usually one fish and one meat, and usually one gourmet style meal along with the other more simple fare. Lobster is a regular feature of the menu, which also includes chicken piccata and shrimp Parmesan. Bill recommends his she-crab soup.

The dining room is small, seating only eighteen, but it has newly restored Rufus Porter murals. A dinner by candlelight here is a treat.

The inn's old tavern is across the hall from the dining room, and although there is no liquor license, setups are provided. The tavern, with Franklin stove and stenciled floor, old paneling and lots of books and games, is a comfortable room in which to relax after dinner.

Temple is another of those lovely Monadnock region villages. Across the street from the inn and adjacent to the village green are the school, library, church, country store, and a couple of old houses. The whole business, including the inn, is part of a historic district. Thoreau visited the inn in 1852; he would probably see few changes in the village if he came back today. And the inn is open again, freshly decorated, quaintly furnished, and as much of a home to travelers as it always has been.

Open all year. No charge cards or pets, BYOB. No dinner on Monday. Temple is on Route 45 just south of Route 101 east of Peterborough.

ACCOMMODATIONS: B & B $24 - $30
                  Dinner $9 - $12

VERMONT

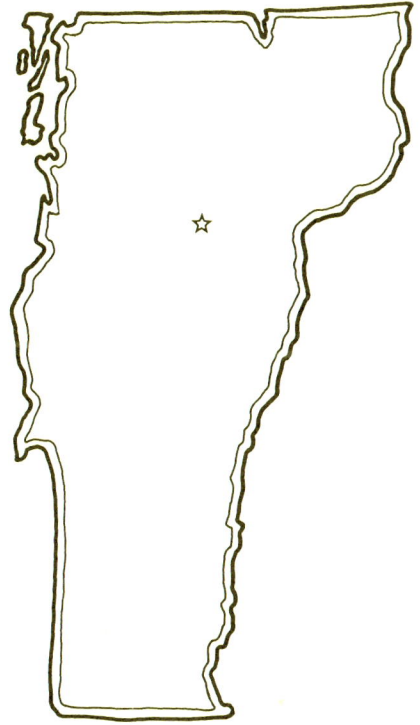

Vermont

1. **ARLINGTON** West Mountain Inn
2. **ARLINGTON VILLAGE** Arlington Inn
3. **BRANDON** Churchill House Inn
4. **BRIDGEWATER CORNERS** The October Country Inn
5. **BROWNSVILLE** The Inn at Mt. Ascutney
6. **CHESTER** Chester Inn
7. **CHITTENDEN** Tulip Tree Inn
8. **CRAFTSBURY** The Craftsbury Inn
9. **CRAFTSBURY COMMON** The Inn on the Common
10. **CUTTINGSVILLE** Shrewsbury Inn
11. **DORSET** Barrows House
12. **DORSET** Dorset Inn
13. **DORSET** Village Auberge
14. **EAST BURKE** The Old Cutter Inn
15. **EAST MIDDLEBURY** Waybury Inn
16. **GOSHEN** Blueberry Hill
17. **GRAFTON** The Old Tavern at Grafton
18. **GRAFTON** Woodchuck Hill Farm
19. **JAMAICA VILLAGE** Three Mountain Inn
20. **JAY** Jay Village Inn
21. **JEFFERSONVILLE** Windridge Inn
22. **KILLINGTON** The Vermont Inn
23. **LANDGROVE** Nordic Inn
24. **LANDGROVE** The Village Inn
25. **LOWER WATERFORD** Rabbitt Hill Farm
26. **LUDLOW** The Governor's Inn
27. **LUDLOW** Okemo Inn
28. **MANCHESTER** Birch Hill Inn
29. **MANCHESTER** The Inn at Manchester
30. **MANCHESTER** Munson 1811 House
31. **MANCHESTER VILLAGE** Reluctant Panther Inn
32. **MENDON** Red Clover Inn

35 **MORETOWN** Camel Hump View Farm
36 **NEWFANE** Old Newfane Inn
37 **NORTH THETFORD** Stone House Inn
38 **NORWICH** Inn at Norwich
39 **PLYMOUTH UNION** Salt Ash Inn
40 **PROCTORSVILLE** Castle Inn
41 **PROCTORSVILLE** The Golden Stage Inn
42 **PROCTORSVILLE** Okemo Lantern Lodge
43 **QUECHEE** Quechee Inn at Marshland
44 **RIPTON VILLAGE** The Chipman Inn
45 **SAXTONS RIVER** Saxtons River Inn
46 **SOUTH LONDONDERRY** The Londonderry Inn
47 **SOUTH LONDONDERRY** Three Clock Inn
48 **STOWE** Edson Hill Manor
49 **STOWE** Foxfire Inn
50 **STOWE** Spruce Pond Inn
51 **STOWE** Ten Acres Lodge
52 **TYSON** Echo Lake Inn
53 **WAITSFIELD** Knoll Farm Country Inn
54 **WAITSFIELD** Millbrook Inn
55 **WAITSFIELD** Mountain View Inn
56 **WAITSFIELD** Tucker Hill Lodge
57 **WEATHERSFIELD** Inn at Weathersfield
58 **WEST ARLINGTON** Grandmother's House
59 **WEST DOVER** The Inn at Saw Mill Farm
60 **WEST DOVER** West Dover Inn
61 **WESTON** The Darling Family Inn
62 **WESTON** The Inn at Weston
63 **WEST TOWNSHEND** Windham Hill Farm
64 **WILMINGTON** The Hermitage
65 **WILMINGTON** Nutmeg Inn
66 **WILMINGTON** The Red Shutter Inn
67 **WILMINGTON** The White House
68 **WOODSTOCK** New England Inn

West Mountain Inn

Off Route 313
ARLINGTON, VERMONT 05250

Telephone: 802-375-6516

Innkeepers: Wes and Mary Ann Carlson

An inn for some twenty years, this place was a private estate, and it includes 150 acres, a barn and a variety of outbuildings. Situated high on a hillside, the inn overlooks the village of Arlington and the Battenkill River, one of the most famous fishing streams in the world. The grounds have sixty species of conifers planted by a previous owner.

One of the inn's twelve rooms has a fireplace and six rooms have private baths. Several rooms, because of the building's gables, have unusual pine-paneled, cathedral ceilings. The beds are mostly antiques with handmade quilts, and several rooms have super views. There is also a "honeymoon cottage" in the woods by a pond.

Dinner is usually one or two entrées with duck, fish, veal, and beef prepared in a country-gourmet style. Most of the meat is organically raised, the grains are natural as well as the vegetables. Desserts are sweetened with honey and maple syrup.

Wes is a retired school principal and his hobbies of raising African violets and tropical fish add to the charm of this inn. Good innkeepers have enthusiasm, and Mary Ann has enough for two inns. Her friendliness is reflected in the family atmosphere of the inn and the special events that are offered. There's a storytelling weekend and the inn celebrates the Festival of St. Lucia in mid-December, when guests are asked to bring homemade ornaments for the tree.

A potter works in the inn's large barn and guests are often invited to sit at the wheel and learn how to throw a pot. There are about twenty miles of cross-country ski trails, just perfect for walking in the warmer months.

The large living room, accented with Wes's plants and a large fireplace, has plenty of books and games. Mary Ann says it's important for an inn to be a place where people can relax, and that's something you can do here.

Open all year. No dinner served for a few weeks in April. Liquor license. Follow Route 313 west of Arlington for ½ mile, turn left across the river and follow the road up the hill to the inn.

ACCOMMODATIONS: *EP* $35 - $45
Breakfast $4 - $5
Dinner $12 - $14

Arlington Inn

Route 7

ARLINGTON VILLAGE, VERMONT 05250

Telephone: 802-375-6532

Innkeeper: Ron Brunk

You can't miss this imposing Greek Revival mansion right in the middle of Arlington. When the house was built in 1848, the owner's father, Sylvester Deming, considered it ostentatious and tried to burn it down. Happily, he failed, and since 1896 it has been welcoming travelers.

Furnished with exquisite antiques ranging from Oriental rugs to four-poster beds, and accented with signed Norman Rockwell prints, the Arlington Inn is certainly memorable.

The seven guest rooms, plus four others in the

coach house, all have private baths and various combinations of double and twin beds. Each room is named for a person connected with the inn's past. None of the rooms is named for the incendiary Mr. Deming, but it is said that his ghost is occasionally seen walking the halls.

The dining room is beautifully decorated with fireplace and unusual wooden ceiling. During dinner, the whole inn is candlelit and classical music is played.

The cuisine is French, with a number of fish dishes for appetizers, including marinated herring and stuffed clams oregano. Entrées range from steak au poivre and veal picatta to shrimp scampi, chicken Dijon, and seafood crepes. Plan on at least 1½ hours to dine, so just relax and enjoy the atmosphere.

Room rates include a continental breakfast. A brunch with extensive menu is served on Sunday. Before- or after-dinner drinks are available in the small Deming Tavern.

The inn has its own tennis courts, and the Battenkill River, famed for its trout, is just down the street. We have nothing against tennis and fishing, or children, but somehow we think the Arlington Inn is more suited to a special time away for just the two of you.

Open Memorial Day weekend through Thanksgiving weekend. Charge cards, liquor license. Located on Route 7 in Arlington village.

ACCOMMODATIONS: *EP* with continental breakfast
$35 - $59
Dinner $10 - $16.50

Churchill House Inn

Route 73
BRANDON, VERMONT 05733

Telephone: 802-247-3300
Innkeepers: Mike and Marion Shonstrom

This ten-room inn caters to active people who, as Mike says, "want exercise and want to see the countryside." Mike does his best to promote these activities and innkeeping in general with his special and diverse inn-to-inn programs. At the flick of a trout fly, Mike will set up a program for fishermen, hikers and bikers, canoeists, or cross-country skiers for tours lasting from a couple of days up to three weeks. Some twenty inns cooperate with Mike on these primarily self-guided tours. An experienced guide is available for fishing, and the inn rents bikes, skis, and canoes.

Since Mike is also the breakfast cook, he's willing to get up a little early to have breakfast ready for the fishermen. On occasion he will cook breakfast at streamside.

Marion is dinner chef, and her one-entrée, family-style meals range from continental gourmet to traditional New England food. She tries lots of new recipes and entrées may include chicken with a creamy lemon and garlic sauce, Syrian lamb, pork chops with sour pickle sauce, or bouillabaisse. Fresh fish is a specialty and so is the fresh-baked French bread.

The summer rate includes a trail lunch, but you have to ask for it, and soup is served at the inn's cross-country shop in the winter.

Built in 1871, this large, high-ceilinged inn has been run by the current owners for seven years. Five rooms have private baths; the other five share 2½ baths. Furnishings are a combination of Victorian and antique pieces with braided rugs and interesting stenciled floors. One room has a woodstove, and another has a king-size bed.

The living room is large with sofas, Franklin stove and a piano that Mike occasionally plays. Be sure to ask for the details of Mike's inn-to-inn tours.

Open from the beginning of trout season through foliage season, during ski season. Charge cards, beer and wine license. From Route 7 in Brandon, take Route 73 east to the mountains. The inn is on the left beside a stream.

ACCOMMODATIONS: *MAP* $72 - $90

The October Country Inn

Route 4

BRIDGEWATER CORNERS, VERMONT 05035

Telephone: 802-672-3412

Innkeepers: Ruth and Pete Hall

Pete was living in this 150-year-old farmhouse when he met Ruth, who was leading bicycle tours. They began remodeling and modernizing the building for their home. Eventually they decided to open it as an inn.

The Halls have built three additions in the past six years, the latest change a new kitchen and expanded living quarters for themselves. The inn has eight guest rooms including one large room with eight beds used mainly for groups. There are five hall baths for the eight rooms.

Dinners are served family-style with candlelight and

complimentary wine. The one-entrée meals feature homemade breads, soups, and desserts, and vegetables from the inn's garden. Many international entrées plus standard American fare are offered in winter, with lighter meals featuring plenty of home-grown vegetables in summer. Usually in summer a second vegetarian entrée is offered. Breakfast is served every day with eggs, pancakes, French toast, and bacon.

The inn has a large living room with a huge old woodstove that heats most of the building. There are lots of games and books, and sports fans might want to ask Pete about baseball. Killington ski area is nearby and several bike tours use this inn as an overnight stop.

Open December to April; late May to October. No dinner on Wednesdays. No charge cards, BYOB. The inn is on a short road that parallels the village of Bridgewater Corners. Their sign is on a barn that can be seen from Route 4.

ACCOMMODATIONS: *MAP* $55 - $60

The Inn at Mt. Ascutney

BROWNSVILLE, VERMONT 05037

Telephone: 802-484-7725

Innkeepers: Eric and Margaret Rothchild

Each inn has special things to offer, and here one is first overwhelmed with the view. Situated high on a hillside surrounded by fields, this inn has commanding vistas — especially of Mt. Ascutney, which seems to rise out of the front yard.

Enter the main dining room and you'll have another surprise. The kitchen is part of the dining room, and Margaret, who is a graduate of the Cordon Bleu school and has conducted her own cooking demonstrations for years, prepares all the meals before the diner's eyes. She enjoys chatting with guests as she works, and for those who have never watched a professional chef this is a real treat.

Margaret describes her menu as country cooking with a continental flair. Entrées include duck with olives, Persian lamb, shrimp Florentine, and spiced scrod — scrod coated with ginger and paprika, baked on a bed of onions with white wine. New England boiled dinner, lasagna, and steak are also offered.

For dessert try Chocolate Ascutney, a pound cake that looks like the mountain and features three liqueurs and pecans. Margaret is also a trained pastry chef.

The dining room and small bar are located in what was once the stable and carriage house of the 170-year-old farm. Attached is the farmhouse with its six guest rooms, living room with fireplace, and a small breakfast room. It is arranged so that house guests have the place to themselves while dinner guests use a separate entrance to the restaurant. A restaurant since 1971, the business was expanded to an inn when the Rothchilds came in 1979.

Four of the guest rooms are large, with private baths, quilts made by Margaret, and traditional furnishings. The other four rooms share two baths.

Eric, who occasionally cooks breakfast, is building a varied wine list and boasts of having representation from each wine valley in France. Ask him about their new solar home.

Open May through October; December through March. Liquor license, children, charge cards, pets by advance permission. From Exit 8 on I-91, take Route 5 north to Route 44. The inn is on a side road across from the Mt. Ascutney Ski Area entrance. Follow this side road up a steep hill to the inn.

ACCOMMODATIONS: $35 - $52 with breakfast and afternoon tea
No dinner on Tuesday and Wednesday

Chester Inn

Route 103

CHESTER, VERMONT 05143

Telephone: 802-875-2444

Innkeepers: Tom and Betsy Guido

This big old inn has anchored the center of this little town for over a hundred years. Tom and Betsy came to Vermont from Ohio, where he was an insurance executive. They were looking for a small business to buy and stayed at this inn while they looked. Three months later, they were the owners.

That was five years ago, and they have worked hard to make their mark on this historic place. A number of fine antiques and paintings, some from Betsy's father's collection, accent the large living room and dining room. Tennis courts, heated pool, sauna, and exercise room are all available for active guests. There are rockers on the porch for the less energetic.

Part of this building housed a bank, and this section — complete with vault — has recently been converted to Van Gogh's Pub, with a more contemporary atmosphere than the rest of the inn. Lunch is served here daily, and there is music in the evening.

Chester Inn has thirty-one rooms, each with private bath, and some rooms are connecting to accommodate family groups.

The large dining room is traditional in style with pewter accessories, exposed beams, and several fine antique cupboards. The menu, though, is continental. Duck with peaches (flamed at your table), beef Bourguignonne served in a copper casserole, chateaubriand bearnaise for two, pheasant, and locally raised veal are among the house specialties. Usually four to five entrées are offered nightly. Soups (including fresh tomato) and French bread are made at the inn.

Lunch is served Monday through Friday, but the main dining room is closed on Monday except during holiday weeks.

Chester has lots of antique shops and Tom will suggest places for short walks or hikes. Don't miss the lovely stone village nearby in Chester Depot, or the old meetinghouse in Rockingham.

Open mid-November through March; Mother's Day through October. Liquor license, charge cards. From exit 6 on I-91, follow Route 103 to Chester and the inn.

ACCOMMODATIONS: B & B $40 - $52
                 Dinner $10 - $14

Tulip Tree Inn
Chittenden Dam Road
CHITTENDEN, VERMONT 05737

Telephone: 802-483-6213

Innkeepers: Ron and Fini Schutz

This rambling country house was built by Frederick Barstow, a business partner of Thomas Edison, but it has been a country inn for about eight years. Surrounded by forest and entered by crossing a small brook, the inn is picturesque in any season, but it was especially inviting on the winter night that I arrived.

Somewhat off the beaten path but easily reached off Route 7 north of Rutland, the inn has ten rooms, two with private baths and the rest sharing a bath for each two rooms. Rooms vary in size and shape, and the furnishings include a variety of antiques and old bed frames.

Ron, who is a retired New York policeman, is the bartender, maintenance man, and baker of breads, rolls, cakes, and pastries.

Fini runs the rest of the kitchen. She specializes in continental cooking, offering one-entrée dinners that include veal picatta, chicken Cumberland, and butterflied leg of lamb. Appetizer, salad, and rich dessert round out the menu. The full breakfast varies from eggs to pancakes. Guests are served family-style at three large tables in the dining room.

The inn has two living rooms, one with a woodstove. The other, much larger and pine paneled, has a stone fireplace, large windows, and plenty of games and books. The original library is now the taproom, a recent addition to the inn.

The inn has its own swimming pool, and groomed cross-country trails are nearby. Tulip Tree and the Red Clover Inn in nearby Mendon offer inn-to-inn cross-country skiing. Ask for details.

The road to the inn deadends not far up the hill at the Chittenden reservoir, which is well known for its excellent fishing.

Open all year except for April and November. No charge cards, liquor license. From Route 4 west of Sherburne Pass or Route 7 north of Rutland, watch for the inn's sign.

ACCOMMODATIONS: *MAP* $76 - $90

The Craftsbury Inn

CRAFTSBURY, VERMONT 05286

Telephone: 802-586-2848
Innkeepers: John and Susan McCarthy

Craftsbury is one of those small villages tucked away in Vermont's Northeast Kingdom. In years past, every village had a wealthy landowner who built an imposing home right in the center of town. The Craftsbury Inn, built in the Greek Revival style about 1850 for merchant Amasa Scott, retains the beauty and architectural style specified by Mr. Scott.

The columns of the facade allow space for a second-story porch offering views of the country store and the white houses and colorful gardens of the town. Bird's-eye maple woodwork and embossed tin ceilings accent the interior. Wide pine floors, beautifully finished, and the living room antiques and fireplace add to the charm of this old building.

The chef is a graduate of the Johnson and Wales Culinary Institute. The dining room, with large windows opening to the gardens of the spacious yard, is open to the public by reservation.

The continental menu features three entrées per evening, changed daily, and everything is cooked from scratch, including breads and ice cream.

A typical meal begins with appetizer, then homemade soup, a salad (perhaps watercress with mushrooms), entrée, then dessert of two or three kinds of ice cream, chocolate mousse, or pastry. Lamb chops with fresh mint sauce, veal Marsala, chicken diablo, and fresh fish are among menu entrées. Overnight guests are offered a full breakfast.

The inn has nine comfortable rooms, each bed with a handmade quilt. Two rooms have private baths while the others share hall baths. There is a small TV room and a lounge just off the well-equipped bar.

Craftsbury is a quiet village, perfect for those who want to read away a weekend. For the more active, nearby Greensboro has a large lake and there are miles of good bicycling roads.

Closed November and April. Restaurant is closed on Mondays. No charge cards, liquor license, children 9 and over, pets by advance request. From exit 7 on I-89, follow Route 2 to Route 14 and watch for the sign to Craftsbury. The inn is in the center of the village.

ACCOMMODATIONS: B & B $45 - $60
                 MAP $70 - $85

The Inn on the Common

CRAFTSBURY COMMON, VERMONT 05827

Telephone: 802-586-9619

Innkeepers: Penny and Michael Schmitt

Picture a small village with fenced common and houses fronted with white picket fences, and you'll describe Craftsbury Common.

Such a setting requires a special inn and the Inn on the Common is precisely that. Frequent summer vacationers in the area, the Schmitts moved up from New York and opened the place eight years ago. The main house was tastefully restored and in the intervening years, they have added a second house across the country road, a swimming pool, clay tennis court, formal gardens, a lovely crafts shop, and — Michael's pride —

an English croquet court. English croquet is different from the usual backyard game and requires skill and a thorough knowledge of the rules, especially if one expects to defeat Michael.

For those who seek the country to exercise, the inn is affiliated with the Craftsbury Sports Center, which offers expert training in kayaking, canoeing, and running in the summer and cross-country skiing in the winter. Inn guests have free use of skis and the trails. Lake swimming and nature walks are also offered in season. This is also great birding country.

The inn has fifteen rooms, five with private baths and five shared baths for the other rooms. Each room has handmade Vermont quilts, thick terry cloth robes for "going down the hall" and traditional decor with a few contemporary accents. Three rooms have woodstove fireplaces and others are extra large with easy chairs and sofas.

Before-dinner drinks are served in the library. In winter enjoy the roaring fire, but in warmer weather guests often join the hosts for a game of croquet before dinner.

Although Penny oversees the kitchen, she and Michael sit with their guests at two large tables for dinner. The evening meal is the day's focal point and guests often dine for two hours, enjoying the varied and unusual food and the complimentary wine that Michael pours. The one-entrée meals include such items as lamb with sorrel sauce, cold veal with fish sauce, or shrimp and dill. The Schmitts grow some of their own vegetables and most of the herbs. Soups, salads, breads, and desserts complete the menu.

After dinner tea and coffee are served in the living room, and the hosts urge their guests to take a walk around the common before turning in for the night.

On the second floor of each building is a sitting room with television and lots of books and magazines, but with so much to see and do in the area, we doubt that the TVs get much use.

Breakfast is more than ample, with cereals, many kinds of eggs, and fresh breads. For those who need lunch, there is a small kitchen for guests to use.

The Schmitts certainly provide a positive answer to the question, "Can an inn start from scratch in a small rural town miles from the nearest turnpike and be successful?"

Open the weekend before Christmas through mid-March; mid-May to the Sunday after Columbus Day. Charge cards, liquor license, children under 4 and pets by arrangement. Take exit 7 on I-89 at Montpelier and follow Route 2 to Craftsbury and the inn. From St. Johnsbury take exit 21 off I-91 and follow Route 2 to Danville, then Routes 15 and 14 to Craftsbury Common.

ACCOMMODATIONS: *MAP* $80 - $110

Shrewsbury Inn
Route 103
CUTTINGSVILLE, VERMONT 05738

Telephone: 802-492-3355

Innkeepers: Lois and Don Butler, Kerry and Gilbert Dillon

The Butlers, with sons Kerry and Gilbert, opened this inn about a year ago. The renovations have been extensive, and the result is a richly furnished and decorated hostelry. Lois's extensive collection of English brass rubbings accent and set the tone for the decor, especially in the bedrooms, where the tester beds are both unusual and attractive. Other antiques and art from the Butlers' former home reflect their travels throughout the world.

The inn has six bedrooms, two singles and four

large rooms, all with twin beds. A three-bath, three-shower complex serves all bedrooms.

Gilbert, an experienced cook, sets up the menu, and it reflects his continental tastes. Six to eight entrées change regularly and may include shrimp Pierre, veal Gilbert, clams Roberto, or chicken stuffed with ham and mushrooms in a sour cream sauce.

The dining room with its marble fireplace is open to the public Tuesday through Saturday, and lunch is served from June through foliage season. A full breakfast is served to house guests only.

The inn has a small pub and a cozy living room with another marble fireplace. Built in the 1830s, the brick building was remodeled about 1900, perhaps around the same time that the nearby Haunted Mansion Book Shop was constructed. With that name, who wouldn't be tempted to visit?

Open all year except for April and November. Charge cards, liquor license, no children under 4. From Route 7, follow Route 140 and Route 103 to the village of Cuttingsville.

ACCOMMODATIONS: B & B $36
                 Dinner $9 - $13

Barrows House
Route 30
DORSET, VERMONT 05251

Telephone: 802-867-4455

Innkeepers: Charlie and Marilyn Schubert

    The Barrows family turned this 200-year-old building into an inn in 1900, and the Schuberts, who have been here for about ten years, have continued the innkeeping tradition while expanding the facilities and accommodations.

    The latest touch is a beautiful white gazebo set off to one side of the six-acre grounds and lighted at night. Two tennis courts and a swimming pool keep summer guests occupied when the inn has its busiest season.

    The inn has ten rooms in the main building and a total of seventeen rooms in several cottages clustered on the grounds. The cottages vary, and some have kitchenettes, fireplaces, bunks, and private sitting rooms. Almost all rooms have private baths, and furnishings vary from antiques to newer pieces. The rooms have comfortable chairs and reading lamps.

Meals are served in a large dining room, formally appointed with many fine paintings and prints on the walls. The menu is basically continental, with six or seven entrées offered nightly. The inn rotates seven menus so that guests staying for a week — as many do — have new choices every day.

Veal Morengo, chicken Kiev, pork sautéed with apples and white wine, scallops Provençale, and coq au vin are only some of the entrées available. Fish and meat specialites are offered daily as well. The vegetables are also served with an extra touch: sautéed cucumbers with dill and sour cream, peas with mint, and potatoes Chantilly. Homemade bread, appetizers, salad, and dessert are included. Breakfast features blueberry and apple pancakes as well as various eggs and cereal. Lunch is served from summer through the foliage season.

Before and after-dinner drinks are available in the cozy tavern. The inn's living room has a fireplace, books, and lots of magazines. The red clover and the hermit thrush are official symbols of Vermont, and Charlie has adopted them for the inn as well. The pretty flower and secretive bird are worked into the decor as paintings and even on needlework pillows made by the guests.

Open all year. No charge cards. Liquor license. Located right on Route 30 in Dorset village.

ACCOMMODATIONS: *MAP* $100

Dorset Inn
Route 30
DORSET, VERMONT 05251

Telephone: 802-867-5500
Innkeeper: Fred Russell

The main portion of this building was constructed as a tavern before 1800, making this the oldest continuously run inn built as an inn in Vermont. In his twelve years here, Fred has continued the tradition of hospitality. Now with forty-five rooms, all with private baths, the Dorset Inn is right in the middle of Dorset Village fronting on a small green and just across from the country store.

The front section of the inn is the oldest. Here, wide pine floors, low ceilings, and lovely stenciling in one of the two living rooms accent the antiquity.

The guest rooms vary in size, but all reflect a homelike atmosphere, with twin and double beds and plenty of chairs. Comfortable chairs in the guest rooms, to my way of thinking, are nearly as important as comfortable beds.

There are two dining rooms featuring home-style cooking, with about five entrée choices for dinner. Roasts, steaks, chops, and chicken are specialties. During the summer, twenty meals are served weekly and all are available to the public. In addition to breakfast and dinner, a buffet lunch is available. In winter the inn is open on weekends and holiday weeks. Two meals on Saturday and one on Sunday are served buffet-style. On Wednesdays during the summer, the inn offers a cookout with steak and a complimentary cocktail party.

The inn has two small bars and a game room. Just down the street is the Dorset Playhouse. The inn has its own swimming pool and provides golf to guests at the adjacent country club. Ask about the special two-day playhouse and golf packages. Or, just come and sit in the rocking chairs on the front porch and watch the village of Dorset.

Open daily from late May to late October. Open weekends and holiday weeks from Christmas to mid-March. No charge cards, liquor license, small well-behaved pets allowed in certain rooms. From Manchester Center, follow Route 30 to Dorset village green and to inn.

ACCOMMODATIONS: *MAP* $56 - $65

Village Auberge
Route 30
DORSET, VERMONT 05251

Telephone: 802-867-5715

Innkeepers: Alex and Hanneke Koks

Stay at one of several inns in this area, but certainly reserve at least one night for dinner at Village Auberge. (The rooms here equal those of any quality inn, but the focal point is the food.) Alex and Hanneke have been in the restaurant business most of their working lives. In fact, Alex was trained in hotel management in his native Holland, and he has run restaurants there and in Vermont. Hanneke is the hostess.

The menu is continental and Alex changes it several times each year, although rack of lamb and sweetbreads aux morilles are always offered. Chicken breasts à la

Parme, Cornish hen and sauté of veal aux girolles poivres are other special entrée offerings. Daily specials feature fresh fish in season. Appetizers include a duck terrine, a lobster or fish pâté, and escargots. Mustard cream soup is the house specialty among the soups. All desserts are homemade, including a chocolate Grand Marnier cake and a gorgonzola-stuffed pear. The wine list is varied, with emphasis on chateau bottlings from Europe and California.

The dining room is closed on Monday throughout the year, and on Tuesday during the winter. Breakfast is served to house guests only. Dinner reservations are required.

This old farmhouse had been an inn at various times when the Koks bought it in 1978. The building was completely remodeled and there are now six large guest rooms, each with private bath. There is a single three-room suite, and all rooms have wall-to-wall carpeting. Most furnishings are antiques. Beds include twins, doubles, and king size.

The bar is small, but attractive. Swimming, golf, and tennis are available nearby.

Children are welcome, but the Kokses stress that this is not a family inn, and has few on-premises amusements for young guests.

Open May 15 to November 15, December 15 to April 15. Charge cards, liquor license. Located right on Route 30 just south of Dorset village.

ACCOMMODATIONS: *EP* $40 - $55
Dinner $9 - $16

The Old Cutter Inn

Burke Mt. Access Road
EAST BURKE, VERMONT 05832

Telephone: 802-626-5152

Innkeepers: Fritz and Marti Walther

The old house was a playground for squirrels when it was purchased by the owners of the new Burke Mountain ski area a few years ago and renovated as a small inn. Now owned by the Walther family, The Old Cutter Inn is a refreshing change from most lodgings found near ski areas.

Fritz's restaurant experience belies his youthful appearance. Trained for two-and-a-half years through the apprenticeship program in his native Switzerland, Fritz has cooked in a score of restaurants and major hotels in

Europe and America. He spent several years in Stowe and Boston before deciding he was ready to have his own place. After four years here, he has finally developed the kitchen facilities to meet his demanding standards. Guests enter the inn adjacent to the open kitchen door, and they are welcome to watch this third-generation chef and his crew.

Veal Picatta and tournedos of beef Old Cutter Inn are specialties, but duckling, Chateaubriand for two, stuffed shrimp, and sole Duglere are tempting as well. The menu changes a bit during the seasons, and one or two specials are usually offered.

The dining room with fireplace and exposed beams takes up most of the main section of the house. A small tavern, again with fireplace and a small bar, also serves a light menu.

The inn has four rooms in the main building, sharing two baths and a separate shower room, and five bedrooms with private baths in the adjacent carriage house. For beds, most rooms have two doubles, three twins, or a double and a twin. Wide pine floors and exposed beams accent many of the bedrooms.

This inn is one of the most remote we have listed, and its Northeast Kingdom location makes the most of the surrounding woodlands and mountains. Views to the west focus on Willoughby Gap and its eight-mile-long lake. Locals refer to the area as Little Lake Lucerne, and Fritz is quick to agree. Burke Mountain, with its demanding slopes, is one of the state's least commercial ski areas. It's a skier's mountain and Fritz is on the slopes as often as possible. There's a nine-mile cross-country trail leading from the inn's back door and in summer there's plenty of hiking and good bicycling.

Not far from Montreal, the inn's many French Canadian guests and Fritz's continental friendliness create an international atmosphere.

Open Mother's Day through October, early December to early April. Charge cards, liquor license, pets. Exit I-91 at Lyndonville and follow Route 114 to East Burke and the Burke Mountain ski area. The inn is on the left just beyond the first entrance to the ski area.

ACCOMMODATIONS: *EP* $36 - $56
                                Dinner $7.25 - $13

Waybury Inn
Route 125
EAST MIDDLEBURY, VERMONT 05740

Telephone: 802-388-4015

Innkeepers: Dan and Mary Ann Phillips

The Phillipses are transplanted Californians who thought about running an inn for thirty years before buying this historic hostelry a year ago. Built in 1810 as a stagecoach stop, this inn has been serving the traveler ever since.

There are eleven guest rooms, five with private baths, the others sharing one bath for each two rooms. Furnishings are eclectic, with many antiques including a variety of old chests and desks.

A collection of old spinning antiques accents the dining room with its exposed beams. The menu is basically American, with steaks, ham, and lamb featured. Nightly specials include a variety of international dishes. Fresh seafood, including lobster, halibut, and salmon is featured from summer through foliage season. Lunch is served (except in winter), and brunch is a Saturday specialty. Children's dinner portions are available by request. There is also summer dining on the porch.

The Knotty Pine tavern includes the bar, and adjacent is the club room used for special functions. The front parlor is spacious with a large fireplace, Oriental rugs, and comfortable sofas. We can just picture Robert Frost, who lived a few miles away, chatting with guests here before dinner.

Open all year. Charge cards, liquor license. From Route 7, follow Route 125 to the end of East Middlebury village.

ACCOMMODATIONS: *EP* $28 - $38
                  Dinner $5 - $12

Blueberry Hill
RFD 3
GOSHEN, VERMONT 05733

Telephone: 802-247-6735

Innkeepers: Tony and Martha Clark

This is one of New England's premier cross-country ski centers. In fact, the inn was closed during the summer until just two years ago.

Tony runs the ski program, which includes grooming forty miles of trails, traveling by van to local schools to teach skiing, regular weekend ski races, and the 60-km American Ski Marathon — the longest ski race in the country. The touring center has a sales and rental shop, a warming room with hot soup, and beginner instruction. As Tony says, "We're interested in helping people to ski better."

In the summer, however, except for a few weekend running clinics and the 10-km Goshen Gallop, Blueberry Hill is dedicated to relaxation. There's a small pond nearby, and excellent fishing, but summer is the season to just enjoy the atmosphere of the inn itself.

There are seven guest rooms plus a small cottage, all with private baths, furnished with many antiques, and with homemade quilts on the beds. Fresh flowers in the bedrooms are grown by Martha in her rustic greenhouse just off the kitchen. Morning coffee is often served here in the greenhouse among the fragrant blossoms.

Martha runs the kitchen. One-entrée meals vary considerably, and include roast beef with Yorkshire pudding, or roast duck. Quiche and homemade soups and breads are specialties. The dinners are served at one large table, with Tony joining the guests to help everyone get acquainted. Children are often served first at their own table in the kitchen. A full breakfast is offered, and hot drinks and baked goodies are always available in an alcove just off the kitchen.

The living room is large, with fireplace, lots of books, deep sofas, and beautiful dried flowers hanging from the exposed beams.

Blueberry Hill's active ski-touring program keeps the place hopping in the winter, but its country location is just fine for relaxing during the hot weather of summer.

Open mid-December to mid-March, Memorial Day to mid-October. Charge cards, BYOB. From Routes 7 or 100, follow Route 73 to Goshen then take the dirt road north toward Ripton. Watch for Blueberry Hill signs.

ACCOMMODATIONS: *MAP* $95

The Old Tavern at Grafton

GRAFTON, VERMONT 05146

Telephone: 802-843-2231

Innkeeper: Lois M. Copping

The term *country elegant* could be coined to describe the Old Tavern. It is unlike any other inn in this book for a number of reasons. Although nearly two hundred years old, the building was completely renovated from the exterior walls in during 1966 by the Windham Foundation, a non-profit historical preservation foundation that has renovated many of the buildings in this small village. Some of these buildings have been sold after restoration but other structures, including The Old Tavern, two houses used for an annex, and six guest houses, have been retained and are open to guests.

The inn itself has fourteen rooms and the annex (really two delightfully restored and furnished houses) just across the street has twenty more rooms each with private bath. Most of the rooms have twin beds although there are some doubles with canopy beds. Four guest houses rent by the day (for the entire house), and they sleep seven to nine guests, making them perfect for a large traveling family. Small children and pets are welcome in two of the guest houses.

All of the living rooms and bedrooms are exquisitely furnished with antiques. Old chairs, paintings, pewter and Colonial architecture combine handsomely. An elevator serves the inn's three floors.

The three dining rooms (jackets required for dinner and no cigars or pipes, please) fit the diners' various moods. In the evening the formal dining room, with its china and crystal, creates the proper atmosphere. Grafton is only a village, without evening entertainment available, so dinner at the Tavern becomes the evening event.

The tavern dining room, with its fireplace and pine paneling, is less formal, and the new dining room with skylights and a greenhouse opening to a formal garden "patio" is delightful for any meal.

The inn's three meals daily cover everything from good country cooking to more continental specialties such as veal Oscar, or crepes Saint Michel. Steak and seafood are featured. Menus change daily and the wine list is varied and not too expensive.

In the remodeled barn is a bar and large fireplace. Here a balcony room has a few games and the inn's only television.

Signing the guest register here puts one in the company of Thoreau, Emerson, Daniel Webster, Hawthorne, and Kipling, for whom one living room is now named.

Open all year except for Christmas Eve and day, and April. No charge cards, liquor license, children under 7 and pets in two guest houses only. From exit 5 off I-91, follow Route 121 to the village of Grafton.

ACCOMMODATIONS: *EP* $35 - $70
Dinner $8.25 - $12.50

Woodchuck Hill Farm
Middletown Road
GRAFTON, VERMONT 05146

Telephone: 802-843-2398

Innkeepers: Anne and Frank Gabriel

This lovely 1780 farmhouse, beautifully furnished and reached by following a winding dirt road, is the Gabriels' home most of the year. In the warmer months they welcome guests, many of whom are repeat visitors, to their quiet place in the country.

The house has four large, corner guest rooms, a studio apartment with kitchenette, and a charming remodeled barn, also with kitchen, that sleeps four. There is a large common room with fireplace for guests, and setups are served here nightly. There is no liquor license, so bring your own beverages.

Dinner is served to house guests by reservation and is a one-entrée meal prepared by Ann. Grilled trout from the farm pond, scallops Provençale, lemon chicken, and leg of lamb are among the many entrées served. The continental breakfast features bran muffins and blueberry boy bait (a breakfast coffee cake, or a dessert when topped with whipped cream).

Part of the barn is a nice antique shop with all of those interesting items you would expect to find on a back road in Vermont.

Behind the barn is the trout pond — good for swimming, too — and a pretty white gazebo. There are lots of roads for walking, but for sheer pleasure and relaxation, don't miss the porch with its wicker furniture and seventy-five-mile view across the hills of Vermont and New Hampshire. We'll not soon forget an afternoon here with a cold beverage, Grafton cheese and crackers, watching hummingbirds at the flowers.

Open May through October. No charge cards or liquor license. Children over 8. Take exit 5 off I-91 and follow Route 121 to the village of Grafton. Drive past the Old Tavern, and continue straight on Main Street up the hill to where the pavement ends. Follow "Gabriel's Barn Antiques" signs for another two miles.

ACCOMMODATIONS: *EP* with continental breakfast $38
Dinner by reservation $15

Three Mountain Inn
Route 30
JAMAICA, VERMONT 05343

Telephone: 802-874-4140

Innkeepers: Charles and Elaine Murray

Anyone would feel at home in this 1780 inn. The large keeping room, once the old kitchen, is now the living room, and a roaring fire accents the large fireplace and grand piano. The Murrays have learned to cook in the beehive oven, where they bake breads and other food on occasion.

Five of the inn's eight rooms have private baths, and one room has a king-sized four-poster; another room has a small balcony that overlooks the unusual stone swimming pool. There are other rooms in the attached rebuilt stable. Adjacent to the pool is a chalet with two bedrooms, living room, and small kitchen. It rents by the week except in winter.

The dining rooms are small, for intimate dining by candlelight and classical music. Elaine sets up the menus with a focus on homemade items such as the soups (mussel bisque, carrot Vichy), breads (zucchini, dill, carrot), and desserts (cherry cheesecake, Jamaican ice cream).

Entrées change with the seasons to take advantage of the fresh meats and produce. Fresh trout and salmon, three chicken dishes, beef Strogonoff, and vegetable quiche are among the offerings. A specialty is veal Swisse: veal sautéed with shallots, sauced with dry white wine and cream, and served on Swiss rosti potatoes.

About five of these entrées are offered nightly, but the menu changes daily so week-long guests are sure of having a wide variety. The wine list is varied, with French and California wines. The full breakfast includes homemade donuts, pancakes or eggs, fresh sausage, and smoked Canadian bacon.

Jamaica State Park is nearby for hiking and cross-country skiing, and so are several downhill ski areas. The inn's midwinter five-day package is among the most reasonable we have encountered at $139 per person.

Open all year except for the month of April, weekends only in May, and closed sometimes in November until Thanksgiving. Dinner is not served on Wednesday. Charge through Western Union only, liquor license. From exit 2 on I-91, follow Route 30 to Jamaica Village and the inn.

ACCOMMODATIONS: *MAP* $72 - $90

Jay Village Inn
Route 242
JAY, VERMONT 05859

Telephone: 802-988-2643

Innkeepers: Bill and Patricia Schug

If you get a feeling of French culture here there are two reasons. First, Jay is only about five miles from the Canadian border, and many French Canadian guests make the short drive down from Montreal to ski the slopes of nearby Jay Peak. More important, perhaps, is Pat's family (Papa, Mama, brother Michel, and his wife Gigi) who are natives of Paris and all part of the business.

Part of this inn was built about 1900 as a farmhouse, but it was remodeled, with a large addition, in the 1960s when the ski area opened. The inn has fourteen rooms (six with private baths, four two-room suites). Bedrooms have more modern furnishings, are carpeted, and some sleep up to four people.

The lounge has a player piano, large stone fireplace, and a bar decorated with a wide variety of old bottles, antiques, and interesting memorabilia. During the warmer months, drinks are served on the patio surrounding the large swimming pool.

Dinner is served in the large Gallerie D'Art dining room filled with a variety of paintings, lithographs, prints, and photographs. Exquisite antiques here include a tall clock with handmade works, and a cupboard, both from Brittany.

The menu is varied and offers several seafood entrées. Rack of lamb rosemary, shellfish Provençale, steak au poivre, and calves liver Lyonnaise are among the entrées. Parisian bread is baked fresh daily and all items are cooked to order. *MAP* guests do not order from the menu, but are offered one entrée nightly. Complete *MAP* dinners include tarragon chicken, roast sirloin, stuffed fish, or beef kabobs.

Downhill and cross-country skiing are the prime winter attractions. Summer guests might want to make a long day trip to Montreal, hike the Long trail, swim, or boat on nearby lakes.

Open all year except for about a month after the end of ski season. Dining room closed Mondays from late June through foliage season. Charge cards, liquor license, children. From exit 10 on I-89, follow Route 100 through Stowe to Route 101 at Troy, then follow Route 242 to the inn. From the Burlington area, take exit 15 on I-89 and follow Route 15 to Route 100 at Johnson, then follow Route 100 north.

ACCOMMODATIONS: *EP* $27 in summer, $36 - $38 in winter
MAP in ski season $66 - $70

Windridge Inn

JEFFERSONVILLE, VERMONT 05464

Telephone: 802-644-8281

Prop: Alden Bryan

Innkeepers: Berni and Jane Kuntzelmann

Alden Bryan came to this village in 1939 to study painting, fell in love with the place, and has been here ever since. When the Smugglers Notch ski area opened, he decided the area needed a top-quality place to lodge and dine. The Windridge is the result. It has only five rooms, each with private, modern bath, but virtually the entire inn is furnished with English, French, and American antiques. Bryan spent two winters transforming his hundred-year-old building into a restoration of eighteenth-century period. Authentic wide-board paneling and a magnificent corner cupboard are the highlights here.

The restaurant, open to the public, is called The Pullet Room. Behind a glass wall in one of the rooms are real chickens and a few doves contentedly sitting on their nests. The Kuntzelmanns now manage the inn, and they have made some menu changes. Entrées include veal Oskar, steaks, chicken in a béchamel sauce with a hint of curry, baked clams, and other seafoods. Breads and pastries are made next door in the Windridge Bakery. There's a nice wine list, and the inn has a small bar open primarily for dinner and for inn guests. Luncheon is served daily from June through foliage season.

Bryan runs a tennis camp in the summer, and behind the inn are indoor courts that are available for inn guests by special arrangement.

Open all year. Liquor license. Located in Jefferson Village at the junction of Routes 15 and 108.

ACCOMMODATIONS: *EP* $30
                 Dinner $7.75 - $11

The Vermont Inn
Route 4
KILLINGTON, VERMONT 05751

Telephone: 802-773-9847

Innkeepers: Alan and Judy Carmasin

This nineteenth-century farmhouse became a lodge in the 1950s and has been called the Vermont Inn since 1962.

All fourteen guest rooms are different with double and twin beds, carpeting, and most attractive silkscreened fabric wallprints made by a family friend. Eight of the rooms have private baths, and the other six share two large hall baths.

The dining room, with woodstove, fireplace, and large windows with views to Pico Mountain, has a variety of contemporary paintings and prints. The menu, which changes about twice a year, is continental, with veal and seafood specialties. Scallops au vermouth, roast duck Grand Marnier, steak Diane, and tenderloin of pork are among the entrées. Appetizers include escargots and quiche, and the desserts are pleasantly fattening! Judy cooks the full country breakfasts.

The living room, with another woodstove and television, is filled with plants and has other mountain views. There is also a small game room.

Downhill and cross-country skiing are nearby, and for summer visitors the inn has a pool, tennis court, lawn games, and a picnic area by a wooded brook.

Open all year except for May. Charge cards, liquor license. Located just off Route 4, west of Sherburne Pass.

ACCOMMODATIONS: Summer — *EP* with continental breakfast $28 - $38
Winter — *MAP* $66 - $80
Dinner $7.50 - $13.25

Nordic Inn

LANDGROVE, VERMONT 05148

Telephone: 802-824-6444

Innkeepers: Inger Johansson and Filippo Pagano

At a place called the Nordic Inn, one would expect to find a blond, rosy-cheeked innkeeper, Scandinavian food, and cross-country skiing, and that's exactly what you will find here.

Inger is Swedish, is trained in hotel management, and pity the Swedish consul in New York who no longer has Inger as his chef. Actually, her Swedish friends and anyone else who loves Scandinavian food can make the short hop to Vermont and continue to sample her cooking.

Begin dinner with stuffed mushrooms or mussels

Provençale. Then try homemade soup of the day, and for a main entrée, select from salmon baked on a bed of dill with hollandaise sauce, or roast baby lamb in herbal mustard sauce. There is also a variety of continental fish dishes, filet mignon, and chicken à la Inger—chicken breast sautéed in herb butter and topped with bearnaise sauce.

The desserts are downright sinful: hazelnut torte from an old Swedish recipe, crepes filled with almond custard and topped with raspberry sauce, or apples baked in almond butter and cream sauce with lingonberry ice cream.

We'd better not go into further detail about the full breakfast for house guests, Sunday brunch, or lunch, served daily in the pub. With all of this tasty food available, the guest needs some exercise. Behind the inn is a twelve-mile cross-country trail network, and for the beginner there are lessons, sometimes taught by Inger. New equipment and rentals are available in the ski shop.

For those who want to try Nordic techniques on alpine slopes, Filippo has begun the East's only telemark skiing program at nearby Bromley Mountain. The telemark turn, a picturesque technique dating from the pre-metal edge ski era, is a method that allows cross-country skiers to successfully negotiate downhill trails. And if your legs get tired from all of this activity, limber up your arms by joining Filippo for his weekly dart tournaments in the inn's pub. Package plans for both cross-country and telemark programs are offered.

Nordic Inn has five rooms, including an extra-large one with double bed and fireplace. Two of the rooms share one bath. The other three all have private baths. Brightly decorated, the rooms are named for the four Scandinavian countries plus Vermont. This combination of room names does seem appropriate, for Inger has truly brought a Scandinavian atmosphere to New England.

Open all year except for a few weeks at the close of ski season. Charge cards, liquor license. The inn is located on Route 11, midway between Manchester and Londonderry.

ACCOMMODATIONS: *MAP* $87 - $109

The Village Inn
RFD
LANDGROVE, VERMONT 05148

Telephone: 802-824-6673
Innkeepers: The Snyders

Travel a birch-lined dirt road to this inn in the midst of the Green Mountain National Forest. The elder Snyders have been here since 1961, first running the inn during the winter only and then adding a summer season about ten years ago.

The main house was built about 1820, and it includes a few guest rooms plus the dining and living rooms. With the remodeled barn as a lounge, and a 1976 addition of several new guest rooms, The Village Inn rambles from the distant past to the present.

Jay and Kathy Snyder do most of the cooking. Their

one-entrée meals are traditional home-cooked fare, with roast beef and pork, barbecued chicken, baked haddock, or country-style spareribs featured. Don is the breakfast cook, and he prepares enough variety to keep the active skier well fortified throughout the day.

The inn has twenty rooms, eleven of which have private baths. Furnishings are mostly traditional, although the new wing has more modern pieces.

The inn has a new liquor license, and drinks are served in the rustic lounge constructed from the old barn. The wide skiers' couch before the roaring fireplace is the perfect spot for before-dinner relaxing.

Downhill ski areas are nearby, but this is a great place for the cross-country enthusiast. There are miles and miles of trails in the forest, some connecting with the Wild Wing Cross-Country Center. Winter guests will enjoy the newly installed hot tub.

The inn has tennis courts, swimming pool, and four hole, par-3 golf course. And best of all, it has that surrounding forest and an evening stillness that truly relaxes the mind.

Open July through mid-October, late November through March. Charge cards, liquor license, children. From Londonderry, follow Route 11 west one-half mile past the shopping center and turn right on Landgrove Road. Bear left after crossing the bridge and the inn is on the right.

ACCOMMODATIONS: MAP $40 - $76 September 15 through April.
B & B $20 - $40 July through September 15.

Rabbitt Hill Inn

Route 18

LOWER WATERFORD, VERMONT 05848

Telephone: 802-748-5168

Innkeepers: Eric and Beth Charlton

Rabbitt Hill's rambling buildings are an integral part of one of Vermont's prettiest villages. Situated across the street from the church and post office, with views across the Connecticut river to the White Mountains of New Hampshire, Rabbitt Hill is a traditional country inn.

Five of its twenty rooms have fireplaces and one room with a canopy bed is especially charming. All rooms have private baths, and there are various combinations of double and twin beds. Some rooms are in an 1855 wing and others are in the traditionally furnished, adjacent "Briar Patch," originally built in 1795 as a tavern.

The main inn, built in 1825 as a private home, has been welcoming travelers for most of the years since 1843. Wide pine boards, creaky floors, fireplaces, and woodstoves contribute to the old-time atmosphere of Rabbitt Hill.

The dinner menu, however, is anything but old-fashioned. Amid such seasonal specialties as lobster, fish, and scallops is steak farci, a pan-broiled rib steak stuffed with blue cheese, bacon, and pear, with a red wine sauce. Special children's portions are also available.

The inn has its own bar, and on the second floor is a wonderful reading nook with plenty of old books and comfortable chairs.

There's a ski-touring center on the premises and in the summer the inn rents bicycles and canoes. Several downhill ski areas are only a half-hour drive away.

Open all year except for early November and a short time after ski season ends. Located on Route 18, a few miles west of Littleton, New Hampshire or east of St. Johnsbury, Vermont.

ACCOMMODATIONS: *EP* $28 - $50
                  Dinner $7 - $12

The Governor's Inn

86 Main Street

LUDLOW, VERMONT 05149

Telephone: 802-228-8830

Innkeepers: Byron and Melissa Schmidt

Turn-of-the-century governors, seeking to impress one and all with their prestige, built remarkable homes, and several of them have been converted to inns. This is one of them, the former townhouse of Governor Wallace Stickney.

High ceilings, rich butternut woodwork, oak doors, a stained-glass window, and unusual painted slate fireplaces have been enhanced by many plants and careful decorating by this young couple, both of whom have food service backgrounds.

One-entrée meals are served, although an alternative to the main entrée is usually provided. Cornish game hen, Cantonese duckling, and lobster Thermidor are among the twenty-five varied menu offerings. Marinated vegetables, salads, and homemade bread, soups, and desserts are featured. They grow many of their own vegetables and flowers. Meals are served family-style at large tables. Breakfast in bed is provided by request at no extra charge.

Several times during the year, the Schmidts offer special weekend programs. Strawberry, apple, and peach festivals, homemade ice cream specials, suckling pig roasted outdoors, clambakes, and wine tasting are some of these extra events. Write the inn for a complete schedule.

There are ten rooms, six with private baths. Each room has fresh fruit and flowers, candy, terry cloth robes, and comforters. The rooms are recently decorated with Victorian beds and other furnishings. A new library on the third floor offers a peaceful getaway spot.

A living room with lots of plants and the small lounge complete the facilities for guests. Ludlow offers downhill and cross-country skiing in winter and a wide range of summer activities.

Open all year except for a few weeks in November and May. Charge cards, liquor license, children, and pets by advance arrangement. From exit 6 on I-91, follow Route 103 to Ludlow, the inn is in the middle of town.

ACCOMMODATIONS: *MAP* $96
                 EP is available.

Okemo Inn

Route 103
LUDLOW, VERMONT 05149

Telephone: 802-228-2031

Innkeepers: Ron and Toni Parry

One of the earliest houses in the Ludlow area, Okemo Inn was a summer guest house in the early 1900s, became a family home, and has been an inn since 1962. The Parrys came here eight years ago after Ron left the army.

Old-fashioned American cooking is the specialty here, and Ron turns out one-entrée, family-style dinners. Turkey, roast beef, chicken breast, and veal are regular menu items, complemented by salads, homemade soups, breads, and desserts.

The inn has twelve rooms and all but two have

private showers or baths. Family suites for up to six people can be arranged. Wide pine floors accent a variety of old bed frames.

The front parlor, with books and comfortable chairs and sofas, has a fireplace accented with pumpkin pine paneling. Adjacent is the informal lounge with large kitchen fireplace and old iron implements. The dining room, which seats thirty-six, has large tables and plenty of windows for a glimpse of the mountain and ski area that give this inn its name.

Okemo Inn has a separate room for television watching, a sauna, swimming pool, and just across the street are golf and cross-country skiing.

Open June through the end of skiing. Liquor license, charge cards, but prefer cash or checks. Located just off Route 103 north of Ludlow village.

ACCOMMODATIONS: *MAP* $65 - $80

Birch Hill Inn

West Road, Box 346
MANCHESTER, VERMONT 05254

Telephone: 802-362-2761
Innkeepers: Pat and Jim Lee

Recently opened, Birch Hill Inn was Pat's family home for over sixty years. She and Jim had romanticized about running an inn for years, and when their children were off to college they decided the time had come to try their fantasy.

The nearly 200-year-old main portion of the house has been added to several times, and the most interesting addition is the spacious common room with large fireplace, pine paneling, and windows opening to the lovely grounds. Birch trees, pastures, and stone walls add charm to this country location.

There are five guest rooms, one with a working fireplace. Three large rooms have private baths while two smaller ones, each with a sink, share a hall bath. Furnishings are antiques and family pieces and all rooms have recently been decorated.

The spacious entrance hall is open, with graceful stairway and beautiful Federal-style doorway. Guests are served one-entrée meals family-style, and the menu features roast chicken, beef, and lamb, with vegetables from the inn's garden or grown locally.

The inn has a swimming pool and miles of old bridle paths are great for walking or cross-country skiing. A few miles down the road toward Manchester is the Southern Vermont Art Center. There is golf and skiing nearby as well.

Open mid-May to mid-October, December 26 to April. Beer and wine license, children over 6, boarding arranged for pets. Follow Route 7 to Manchester and bear left by the old Equinox Hotel to West Road. The inn is a few miles on the right.

ACCOMMODATIONS: MAP $64 - $76
                 B & B $50 - $62

The Inn at Manchester

Route 7

MANCHESTER, VERMONT 05254

Telephone: 802-362-1793

Innkeepers: Stan and Harriet Rosenberg

Stockbroker Stan and teacher Harriet spent four years looking for a likely place to run an inn before they found this Victorian mansion. As Harriet explains, "We totally renovated every inch," and the result is a comfortable hostelry blending antiques and turn-of-the-century charm with old-fashioned hospitality. A diverse collection of paintings, some contemporary, are a counterpoint to the antiquity

The inn has eleven rooms, three with private baths, and the others share six baths. The bedrooms are carpeted and the old bed frames are accented with lovely quilts. Rooms have twins and doubles, and some have one of each. Linen and towels are color-coordinated. On the third floor are rustic rooms with bunks — fine for people traveling with children.

Harriet is the cook, and she likes to try new recipes. The one-entrée meals are served to house guests only and reflect Harriet's gourmet cooking interests. She makes her own breads, soups, and desserts, and during the summer the vegetables come from the inn's own organic garden. A full breakfast is served, often featuring cottage cheese pancakes with blueberry sauce.

The inn has two living rooms, one with piano and fireplace, plus a game room. There's a new swimming pool and enough lawn and board games to keep anyone busy. Special package plans are available for fishing, hiking, golf, cross-country skiing and crafts such as weaving, pottery, painting and sculpting.

Open all year except for April and November. No charge cards, but deposit arranged through Western Union. Wine and beer license. On Route 7 set back from the highway behind a broad lawn.

ACCOMMODATIONS: MAP $46 - $60
                 B & B $31 - $38

Munson 1811 House

Route 7, Box 207

MANCHESTER, VERMONT 05254

Telephone: 802-362-1811

Innkeepers: The Eade Family

This old building has been an inn for most of its years since 1778, when it was built, and 1811, when it was enlarged. From 1903 to 1938 it was the home of the daughter of Robert Todd Lincoln. Lincoln's own mansion is nearby and open to the public as a historic house.

The Eade family has spruced up the inn considerably with new wallpaper and painting. They left Mary Lincoln's room in shades of lavender, her favorite color. This room opens to a small porch and has a solid marble shower.

There are six guest rooms, including two suites, and

all have private baths. Each room is named for a former resident of the house, and three rooms have fireplaces for use by the guests. Furnishings include many antiques.

Breakfast and lunch are served daily. Coffee cake, hot cereal and breakfast pie are among the morning specialties. Lunch includes homemade soups and breads, with salads featured in summer.

The inn's pub is most attractive, with copper-topped bar, fireplace, and Mercedes Benz memorabilia.

Manchester has been a resort town for years. Just across the green from Munson House is the old, now closed Equinox Hotel. A short drive away are the Orvis fishing equipment company store, the Southern Vermont Art Center, and the auto road to the top of Mt. Equinox.

Open all year except for first three weeks of November and from April to mid-May. No charge cards, liquor license, children over 15, pets welcome. Located on Route 7 in the center of Manchester village.

ACCOMMODATIONS: B & B $39 - $62

Reluctant Panther Inn

MANCHESTER, VERMONT 05254

Telephone: 802-362-2568

Innkeepers: Ed and Loretta Friihauf

A purple inn attracts attention, and that is exactly why this old building got its bright coat of paint. Manchester Village is filled with old white houses but there is no mistaking the Reluctant Panther.

Ed and Loretta have just taken over this inn from its original, longtime owners, and while they have a few changes in mind, the Friihaufs plan to continue the current ambiance and decor.

Although the building is old, the decor is more contemporary, with bright paint and wallpapers and shag rugs, the latter sometimes running up the walls in the bedrooms. Each of the seven rooms has a private bath, telephone, television and alarm clock. We never remember to bring an alarm clock and our watch is cranky, so we appreciate this extra service. Four of the inn's eleven fireplaces are in guest rooms. The honeymoon suite is lavender, with a beautiful brass bed.

There are three dining rooms, one of which is a solarium with glass wall, partial glass ceiling, and lots of plants. You can easily imagine a dinner by candlelight here. The winter breakfast room is done in early American style.

Although the menu is undergoing a few changes, the popular five-course dinner will remain, along with such standbys as blue ribbon steak, brace of quail, rainbow trout, and smoked loin of pork. Public dining is by reservation but breakfast is for house guests only.

A lovely painting of two panthers and "one who isn't" accents the lounge, where imported beers are a specialty. The sitting room, with fireplace, has lots of magazines and comfortable chairs.

Despite the intown location, the Reluctant Panther has a private backyard with an unusual marble patio. Since the patio is situated just off the lounge, drinks can be served here on summer afternoons. This is just the spot to relax after a day of fishing, visiting the Southern Vermont Art Center, or the home of Orvis fishing equipment. For winter guests, downhill and cross-country skiing facilities are nearby.

Open Memorial Day through October, December 5 to April 15. Liquor license, charge cards, no children. Located in Manchester Village on Route 7, just 24 miles above Bennington. Look for the purple house.

ACCOMMODATIONS: *EP* $27 - $40
                              Dinner $14 - $18

Red Clover Inn

Woodward Road

MENDON, VERMONT 05701

Telephone: 802-775-2290

Innkeepers: Dennis and Bonnie Rae Tallagnon and sons

Many couples who run inns do so to allow husband, wife, and children to work together. Dennis was running a New Jersey restaurant when the family decided a change was in order.

The Woodward farm had been a summer estate, then was converted to a sometime ski lodge when this family found it a few years ago. The renovations and redecorations have been extensive, resulting in a charming and comfortable inn. Surrounded by woods and rolling fields, the inn has extensive views to Killington and Pico mountains.

There are miles of trails for hiking, snowshoeing and skiing. Tennis courts are within walking distance. There is an inn-to-inn cross-country program with nearby Tulip Tree Inn in Chittenden. Guests use the pool and a large living room with plenty of games and a huge National Geographic collection.

The two dining rooms, each with a fireplace, are open to the public and offer country French cuisine. Dennis changes the menu daily, with veal, seafood and sweetbreads a la Red Clover as specialties. Dining is by candlelight at small tables, just right for couples on a getaway weekend.

The inn has fifteen rooms, eight with private baths. The main building has ten smaller rooms, each well furnished, and five other rooms a few steps away in the remodeled carriage house. Called "The Plum Tree House," the carriage house is popular with families. Nearby is the old red barn with the family horse.

Open from Thanksgiving to mid-April, Memorial Day to just after foliage season. Located just off Route 4 in Mendon. Watch for the sign. Restaurant open Wednesday through Saturday in summer. Charge cards, liquor license, children, dogs if well behaved.

ACCOMMODATIONS: MAP $60 - $90

The Middletown Springs Inn

on the green

MIDDLETOWN SPRINGS, VERMONT 05757

Telephone: 802-235-2198

Innkeepers: Jean and Mel Hendrickson

This 100-year-old mansion has been restored to its former elegance, thanks in part to the Hendricksons and their period furnishings. A unique three-generation doll collection fills one room and overflows into several others.

The Victorian tradition becomes more evident at dinner, when old oil lamps, family pink Spode and blue Staffordshire china and fine linens welcome guests to one of several large old tables for the one-entrée meals. Stuffed pork chops, ham and chicken breasts in a soufflé, or ham rollups with cheese and spinach are among the offerings. Crab bisque, salad with mandarin oranges, almonds, and red onions, and mint coffee parfait round out a typical dinner. Jean's hot fudge sauce is a special treat. Complimentary wine and sherry are served nightly.

One of the seven guest rooms has a private bath, and each room has velour robes for those sharing baths. Furnishings are comfortable, with lots of old family antiques, rugs, and easy chairs.

Guests may relax in the living room, with its fine book collection and more dolls, or by the woodstove in the library. Lawn chairs under the trees welcome summer guests.

The inn sits on the village green close by the old church, the library, and antique shops. Nearby are the famous springs that were so popular with the wealthy Victorians. The large hotels are now gone, leaving the springs, a quiet village, and this fine old inn.

Open all year. Charge cards, BYOB, children. From Bennington, follow Route 7 to Wallingford, then Route 140 to Middletown Springs.

ACCOMMODATIONS: B & B $56
　　　　　　　　　　Dinner $30 for two

Black Lantern Inn

MONTGOMERY VILLAGE, VERMONT 05470

Telephone: 802-326-4507

Innkeepers: Rita and Allan Kalsmith

The Black Lantern began serving travelers on the Montreal to Burlington stagecoach run in 1803, and back at the turn of the century, when Montgomery was a manufacturing town with 5,000 population, the inn was a popular place. Now Montgomery has just a few hundred residents, but the success of Jay Peak ski area has made it possible for this young couple to renovate the old building and offer a continental menu in the country.

Located only two hours from Montreal, the inn has many French-Canadian and other international guests.

Some evenings the dining room is filled with enough languages to resemble the UN.

About eight entrées are offered nightly for dinner, and the menu may include walnut-crusted sole, marinated broiled lamb, fresh fish, and steak with mushrooms and onions. *MAP* guests receive a complete house dinner and a full breakfast.

Ten of the eleven rooms have private baths, and while some of the rooms are small, all are cozy, with eclectic furnishings and traditional decor. Rooms have twin and double beds and some rooms sleep three people.

The sitting room next to the dining room has comfy sofas and an antique stone woodstove. There is a small TV room and a lounge area with full bar service.

Jay Peak skiing is only a few miles away, and there is cross-country skiing from the inn's back door. This inn is a popular North Country stop for the bike tour groups in warmer weather. Golf, tennis, swimming, antique shops, and hiking are nearby. And if you need the services of a good lawyer, Allan will be happy to help — that is, when he's not in the kitchen with Rita preparing a meal.

Open all year except for a few weeks after foliage and/or ski seasons. Charge cards, liquor license, children, but no pets. From exit 10 on I-89, follow Route 100 to Eden, then follow Route 118 to Montgomery Village. From St. Albans, follow Route 105 to East Berkshire, then Route 118 to Montgomery. The brick inn is right in the middle of the village.

ACCOMMODATIONS: *MAP* winter $55 - $60
 EP $30
 Dinner $7.50 - $11

Camel Hump View Farm
Route 100B
MORETOWN, VERMONT 05660

Telephone: 802-496-3614

Innkeepers: Jerry and Wilma Maynard

Camel Hump View Farm is neat, comfortable, and well cared for by the Maynards, who began the inn in 1960. Family living is the accent here, with family-style meals served twice daily in the winter and breakfast only in the summer. Farm-grown vegetables and Wilma's homemade breads, pies, pickles, jams and relishes accent the meals.

Jerry raises beef cattle as a hobby, and he maintains the acre-and-a-half garden.

After dinner, guests gather in the living room to chat or play cards around the dining room tables with their hosts. For many people who come back again and again, staying with the Maynards is like visiting their own relatives in the country. Children are welcome and enjoy the basement game room or the swimming hole in the nearby Mad River.

There are a variety of rooms with bunk and antique double beds, including one two-room suite with private bath just right for a small family. Eight other rooms share four modern baths with showers. Wilma's hand-braided rugs are scattered throughout the house.

Busy in the winter with skiers, the inn is a popular summer spot with bicyclists traveling the length of the state. The latter include foreign visitors from throughout the world.

Open all year, BYOB. From exit 9 on I-89, follow Route 2 to Route 100B. The inn is on the left.

ACCOMMODATIONS: Winter *MAP* $54
  Summer *B & B* $30

Old Newfane Inn
Route 30
NEWFANE, VERMONT 05345

Telephone: 802-365-4427
Innkeepers: Eric and Gundy Weindl

Established in 1787, this is the state's oldest continuously operating inn, and for the past decade it has been known for offering some of the best food in Vermont. Gundy and Eric, who do the cooking, were both trained to cook in Europe and their Swiss-French cuisine is offered in the European style, with careful attention to detail and service.

The menu changes rarely except for specials, but anyone should be happy with duckling in orange sauce, breast of capon Cordon Bleu, escargots Bourgogne, or pepper steak flambé with brandy. Fish and steak are equally interesting.

For a memorable feast, try the rack of lamb or Chateaubriand, both cooked for two and sliced at your table. The service is excellent. The dining room is large, with exposed beams, a roaring fireplace, and accented with ticking clocks and crystal glassware.

The inn has nine guest rooms, seven with private baths, and a continental breakfast is served to house guests. Several of the guest rooms, which are all comfortably furnished and expertly decorated, were once part of the ballroom and have lovely curved ceilings.

The living room runs the full width of the house and, relaxed in an antique sofa with a good book, one could fall asleep here to the ticking of several clocks.

The inn is on the green opposite the old county courthouse and adjacent to several churches, all painted white with green trim. The atmosphere here is thoroughly southern Vermont, but the dining room is unmistakably, deliciously European.

Open mid-May to October, mid-December through March. No charge cards, children over 7 only. From exit 2 on I-91, follow Route 30 to Newfane and the inn.

ACCOMMODATIONS: *EP* $48 - $56
Dinner $9.75 - $17.50
Summer, lunch and dinner;
Winter, dinner only

Stone House Inn

Route 5

NORTH THETFORD, VERMONT 05054

Telephone: 802-333-9124

Innkeepers: Art and Dianne Sharkey

Part of the enjoyment of inns is the variety offered by the innkeepers. Being independent business people, owners set up an inn to suit their own interests. The Sharkeys both like to cook, but not every day. So they offer dinners only on Friday and Saturday, plus holidays such as Thanksgiving, Easter, and Mother's Day.

They prepare a menu, one entrée per day, for a six-week period. Every meal is different and the variety excellent. Borscht and coquilles St. Jacques, vegetable basil soup and roast lamb, oyster bisque and chicken Kiev, and bouillabaisse are only a few selections. Anyway, the menu calendar is printed well in advance, so prospective guests can see what will be offered during their visit. The dining room with fireplace seats twenty-five and is open to the public by reservation. A continental breakfast is included in the rate for house guests.

The inn has only four guest rooms sharing two hall baths. The rooms are well furnished and freshly decorated. Often, small groups or large families reserve the whole place for a weekend.

Before-dinner drinks are served in the two parlors, each with a fireplace. Summer dinners are served on the porch overlooking a small pond that is really an arm of the Connecticut River.

And speaking of the Connecticut River, this inn is the organizer of a new inn-to-inn canoeing program that covers about sixty miles of this river. The program is scheduled for Monday through Thursday and includes three or four inns located beside the river. Canoe rentals are arranged. This really is a stone house. Built in 1835, its walls are many-inches-thick stone blocks.

Open all year. Charge cards. Liquor license. Located just off Route 5, north of exit 14 off I-91.

ACCOMMODATIONS: *EP* with continental breakfast $28
Dinner $6.50 - $12

The Inn at Norwich
NORWICH, VERMONT 05055

Telephone: 802-649-1143

Innkeepers: Al and Doreen Twachtman

This is a bustling village inn because it serves three meals daily and because Dartmouth College is just across the Connecticut River in Hanover, New Hampshire. In fact, Dartmouth folks can easily fill up the guest rooms on football weekends or other times of special events, such as graduation.

This structure was built in 1890, replacing the original 1797 inn that burned in 1889. The Twachtman family has been here since 1979, and they have completely redecorated the downstairs and most of the rooms. Beds, carpeting, and wallpaper are new, and each of the twenty-five rooms has a phone and television. All but two rooms have private baths. Pets are welcome in the separate seven-room motel unit.

Al has many years of restaurant experience, and he is reemphasizing the inn's dining room. All meals are served in the main dining room which has individual tables — candlelit for dinner. There is also terrace dining on the glassed-in porch and a large function room as well. A varied dinner menu includes several cuts of steak, rack of lamb, Cornish game hen, scallops, duck, and rainbow trout.

The inn's bar is tiny, so drinks are served in the large living room furnished with sofas, Oriental rugs, and large fireplace.

Open all year. Charge cards, liquor license, children, pets in motel units. Located just off I-91 in Norwich village.

ACCOMMODATIONS: *EP* $37 - $40
　　　　　　　　　　Dinner $8 - $13

Salt Ash Inn

Route 100

PLYMOUTH UNION, VERMONT 05056

Telephone: 802-672-3748

Innkeepers: Don and Ginny Kroitzsh

This old building began as an inn in the early 1800s, then was the town's post office, general store, and dance hall, and has been an inn again since 1963. Don and Ginny have been here four years, and they run busy foliage season and winter schedules. The summer is quiet.

Meals are served family-style with one entrée. The menu varies and may include veal, roast beef, and pork or lasagna. The breads and desserts are homemade daily.

Four of the eleven rooms have private baths, others

share three hall baths. Since the inn appeals to families and groups, most rooms can accommodate more than two people. Rooms have wall-to-wall carpeting and comfy quilts. Each room is named for former owners rather than numbered. One room is named for former president Calvin Coolidge who was born nearby. About a mile away is the Coolidge birthplace and the Plymouth Cheese factory.

The rustic quality of the inn is most evident in the lounge area, once the post office and general store. The old mailboxes, signs, and other artifacts from the old days are fascinating. In the lounge is a large center fireplace surrounded by sofas, a cozy place to chat with new friends and the innkeepers. An old piano, lots of old books, and board games will keep everyone busy. For the more active, there is skiing nearby and even a few streams where one can pan for gold.

Open weekends in summer then daily in foliage season and mid-December to early April. No dinners on Friday nights. Liquor license, charge cards, pets by special arrangement. Located in Plymouth Union Village at the junction of Routes 100 and 100A.

ACCOMMODATIONS: MAP $56 - $62
EP available

Castle Inn

Box 157

PROCTORSVILLE, VERMONT 05153

Telephone: 802-226-7222

Innkeepers: Michael and Sheryl Fratino

Traditionally, castles were built of stone and situated high on a hill overlooking the village. This unusual inn is no exception to the rule. Built in 1904 by Allan Fletcher, who later became governor of Vermont, the inn is a magnificent example of Victorian aristocratic architecture. The large high-ceilinged rooms of this building have rich dark oak and mahogany paneling with exquisitely detailed plaster ceilings. The richly detailed oval main dining room with its curved walls is as impressive as any dining room that could be imagined.

Michael has been cooking since he was fourteen,

and before acquiring this inn in 1976, he was the chef at a four-star New Hampshire inn where Sheryl was also working.

As befits the atmosphere, the service and menu are continental. Dinner guests are shown to the library by hostess Sheryl, whose friendly manner is a delicate balance to the formal elegance of the building. Cocktails are ordered and served in the library, where guests select their dinner from the menu. When the appetizers are ready, diners are escorted across the hall and seated in one of the two dining rooms. Plan for a leisurely meal. Michael estimates on one-and-a-half hours for two, more time for larger parties. And because of the attention given to each party, reservations for a specific time are requested.

The menu, which changes with the seasons, may include roast duck, capon Mariee, shellfish casino, veal or fish of the day, plus steaks and pork loin. The wine list has been carefully selected from California and European vineyards.

Of the ten guest rooms, nine with private baths, the governor's suite (complete with Governor Fletcher's own bed and dresser) is popular. Mellow sycamore paneling and woodwork accent the upstairs bedrooms and hallways.

Castle Inn has its own hot tub, and for summer guests, a swimming pool and tennis courts.

Open all year except for the end of October through mid-December and from end of skiing season through Memorial Day. Liquor license, children and charge cards. The inn is two miles south of Ludlow, high on a hill at the junction of Routes 103 and 131.

ACCOMMODATIONS: *MAP* $90 - $96

The Golden Stage Inn
Box 218
PROCTORSVILLE, VERMONT 05153

Telephone: 802-226-7744

Innkeepers: Tom and Wende Schaaff

This old rambling house, built at least by 1805, was a stagecoach stop for many years and was once the home of Cornelia Otis Skinner. It has been a full-scale inn since 1974. Tom and Wende took over in 1977 and completely renovated the place. Wende's sister Sue Douglas and her husband Stu ran the Inn at Weston, and they got the Schaafs interested in the inn business.

Wende is the cook, and her recipes are original, featuring some beef, but mainly veal and chicken, which Wende butchers herself. Usually one entrée is offered nightly except when seafood is served. The day we visited, work was nearly completed on Wende's new kitchen. Everything is cooked fresh and to order. Vegetables come from the inn's garden. Tom does the breakfasts.

The dining rooms are small, with tables set for four to enhance the relaxed, intimate dining. Since the building is oriented to the south, light streams in through the large windows and on the small greenhouse addition used for a summer dining room.

The inn has ten rooms, all with double beds, one with private bath and all newly decorated. Nine rooms share five baths. The large windows and recently refinished wide pine floors accent the guest rooms. At the top of the stairs is a small nook with chess set ready to play.

A large living room has a fireplace, fine antique furnishings, and lots of plants. Plenty of skiing is offered nearby, and during the summer the inn is popular with biking groups.

Open all year. Charge cards, children, liquor license. Located just off Route 103 between Chester and Ludlow.

ACCOMMODATIONS: Winter   *MAP* $76
                  Summer   *B & B* $45

Okemo Lantern Lodge
Box 247
PROCTORSVILLE, VERMONT 05153

Telephone: 802-226-7770

Innkeepers: Charles, Joanie, Lisa, and Shon Raciot

Just take one look at this old Victorian village house and you'll fall in love with it. Stained glass windows and natural butternut woodwork recall the elegance of the era. As for Joanie, she's as sweet as Vermont maple syrup and just as much a native. She grew up about eight miles away from the lodge and her father runs the general store across the street. He also smokes the bacon served for breakfast. Joanie's brother is the store's meat cutter, and he takes special care of his sister. Her one-entrée meals are prepared with a gourmet touch. Butterfly of lamb and roast crown of pork are served with home-grown vegetables, home-baked bread and desserts, and homemade jams and other preserves. Dinner is served by candlelight at one of two large old tables.

Breakfast is usually cooked on the kitchen woodstove that Joanie learned to use when she and Charles homesteaded for three years.

The living room is large, with lots of chairs, and an old organ. The inn has six attractive rooms; one with a private bath has a canopy bed. The other rooms have two shared baths and one half bath. Antiques and wicker furniture add to the charm of the bedrooms. For special occasions, plan to have a champagne breakfast in bed.

Afternoon tea is served on the large wraparound porch overlooking the extensive old-fashioned flower garden. To complete the scene, Charles will take you riding in the rumble seat of his restored 1935 Plymouth coupe.

For Joanie, who grew up in a large family and is used to having lots of people around, the lodge is a challenge for the whole family to work at and enjoy. They have been here for only two years but they seem as comfortable with the place as the previous owners who started the inn thirty-three years ago and retired just when this family was interested in taking over.

Open all year. Beer and wine license, charge cards, children. Located on Route 131, just off Route 103 between Ludlow and Chester.

ACCOMMODATIONS: *MAP* $70, children $28 each

The Quechee Inn at Marshland Farm

Box 120, Clubhouse Road
QUECHEE, VERMONT 05059

Telephone: 802-295-3133

Innkeepers: The Yaroschuk family

This is one of those special inns where you'll feel as elegant as the farm's original owner, Colonel Joseph Marsh, who was Vermont's first Lieutenant Governor.

Quechee is the location of one of New England's largest four-season resort communities, and this is of interest to the inn guests who will have privileges at the Quechee Club, which has two golf courses and outdoor tennis courts, plus downhill and cross-country ski areas. The inn has also just opened its own cross-country learning center in the barn.

Each of the twenty-two guest rooms is elegantly furnished mostly with antiques and braided rugs on wide pine floors. Beds are brass and four-poster (would you believe a king-size four-poster?). There are two suites, some rooms are called "deluxe" and others considered "standard," but the only difference seems to be the size of the rooms. All of the rooms are comfortable, each with a private bath and color television, but no ringing telephone.

The original carriage house has been converted to a lounge and sitting area where the continental breakfast and evening cocktails are served. A log fireplace, old beams and barnboard create a pleasant atmosphere where occasionally a musician plays on Saturday evenings.

The dining room is open to the public and offers five or six different entrées nightly. Duck with raspberry sauce, rainbow trout with scallop and crab stuffing, rack of lamb, chicken Bennington, and veal Marsala are among the specialties. Appetizer, salad and vegetables are included in the dinner price. Jackets and reservations are required for dinner.

The inn has a country location across from the Ottauquechee River which offers swimming and canoeing, and just down stream is the deep river-cut Quechee Gorge. A pond wildlife sanctuary is also across the street for birdwatching or canoeing.

Open all year except for two weeks in April and three weeks in early December. Charge cards, liquor license, children. From exit 1 off I-89, follow Route 4 to Quechee and watch for the sign and right turn to Clubhouse Road.

ACCOMMODATIONS: EP with continental breakfast $55 - $80 (mid-May to Nov. 1, Dec. 20 to mid-March); $40 - $60 (mid-March to mid-May, Nov. 1 to Dec. 20) Dinner $11 - $15

The Chipman Inn
Route 125
RIPTON VILLAGE, VERMONT 05766

Telephone: 802-388-2390

Innkeepers: Joan Bullock and family

This is Robert Frost country. The famed poet spent his last years near this small village eight miles from Middlebury. From the west you reach Ripton along the brook-lined Robert Frost Drive and across the Robert Frost Memorial Bridge.

Today would-be poets and writers, participants of the famed Breadloaf conferences, often drop in for the evening. The students and often their more famous instructors entertain themselves with guitars, piano, storytelling and poetry readings. Inn guests are welcome to join in for these impromptu sessions.

The 1823 inn has ten guest rooms, including six with private baths in a recently remodeled woodshed. Most rooms have two or three beds, usually doubles and twins.

Joan brings some of her Pennsylvania Dutch heritage to her cooking. The one-entrée meals, served to house guests only, include cashew chicken, chicken corn soup, lettuce with hot bacon dressing, Cornish game hen, swordfish, and grilled salmon. The living room has plenty of games, puzzles, books, and magazines.

Cocktail hour hors d'oeuvres are served in the tavern with its small bar and large old kitchen-style fireplace. For the energetic, the Middlebury Snow Bowl is nearby along with Lake Dunmore. Or, as Frost might have done, you can stroll on down to the country store and watch the tourists drive by.

Open mid-May through October, mid-December through March. Charge cards, liquor license, children. From Routes 7 or 100, follow Route 125 to Ripton Village.

ACCOMMODATIONS: *MAP* $80

Saxtons River Inn

Main Street

SAXTONS RIVER, VERMONT 05154

Telephone: 802-869-2110

Innkeeper: Averill Campbell Larsen

With a little help from her friends and family, Averill has renovated this old village inn into a delightful hostelry. A native of the town, Averill had run a ski lodge and restaurant in other areas of Vermont. Then she and her Campbell family members decided to buy the old building, which had been built in 1903 as an inn, but more recently had been a private home.

There are twenty-one guest rooms, including four in the restored post-Civil War era house across the street. If your taste runs to vivid colors, you'll love these rooms, which were decorated by Averill's mother. Antique beds, bright wallpaper, plenty of pillows, and reading lamps accent the large rooms.

There are four common rooms for guests, each attractive, and one with television, one for games, and others for just sitting and reading.

Averill is the cook, and her ever-changing menus match the imaginative decor of the guest rooms. Baked shrimp with feta cheese sauce, chicken paprika, Russian vegetable pie, lamb curry, and stuffed halibut steak are typical dinner items. Lunch, also served daily, features several different salads, quiche, crepes, and sandwiches. Averill and her crew make everything here, including the breads.

The inn's lounge is a mixing place for guests and local residents. The bar is topped with copper and the tables include some from an ice cream parlor and others made from old sewing-machine stands.

For guests, Averill has prepared a neat list of things to do including walking trips around the village and countryside and places to drive. You can also visit Averill's brother, who runs the hardware store across the street from the inn.

Averill, who is one of the few natives that we found running an inn, has been here for seven years. It reflects her own style of Vermont hospitality accented with her experiences in foreign travel.

Open daily from April 1 to January 1. Liquor license, no charge cards. From exit 5 on I-91, follow Route 121 to the village and the inn.

ACCOMMODATIONS: EP with continental breakfast
$25 - $45
Dinner $7 - $12

The Londonderry Inn

SOUTH LONDONDERRY, VERMONT 05155

Telephone: 802-824-5226

Innkeepers: Jim and Jean Cavanaugh

    This old house, circa 1826, has a huge living room with a stone fireplace, and adjacent is the dining room seating sixty-five. Patio dining is available in the summer.
    The twenty-five guest rooms have all been redecorated recently, and offer twin and double beds as well as a few kings. Twenty rooms have private baths, and others are part of two-room suites or share baths. There are dorm rooms for boys and girls whose parents are staying at the inn.
    The complimentary breakfast is an innovative buffet complete with soft-boiled eggs and homemade fruit

breads. Dinner menus change nightly, and include specialties such as baked brie, stuffed potato skins, mussels poulette, duckling bigarrade, prime rib of beef, veal goulash, and homemade pastries such as gateau Parisienne or Hungarian rhapsody. No lunch is served in winter.

Guests enjoy aperitifs and after-dinner drinks in the living room around the fireplace in winter and beside the swimming pool in summer. Just off the comfortable bar is a large room with two fine old pool tables — something most inns don't offer.

Situated on a hill in the village, the inn commands a lovely view of the Vermont countryside.

Open all year except short periods after skiing and foliage seasons. No charge cards, liquor license.

ACCOMMODATIONS: *EP* $33 - $50
                  Dinner $9 - $13

Three Clock Inn

SOUTH LONDONDERRY, VERMONT 05155

Telephone: 802-824-6327

Innkeepers: Heinrich and Frances Tschernitz

Heinrich has been a headwaiter in the old tradition all over the world, and he has worked in several southern Vermont resorts and hotels. He says there is no better food to be found anywhere than in this part of Vermont. Modestly, he does not say that his own inn, now in its fourteenth year, is one of the best — but of course it is.

French cuisine in the classic manner is the specialty here. Frogs' legs Provençale, scampi maison, veal scaloppine, piccata, and Marsala are part of this small but exquisite menu. Lamb, duck, and various steaks round out the entrées; herring in sour cream, peppers with anchovy filets, and smoked salmon are among the appetizers. Dining is by reservation only.

There are four small dining rooms, each with small tables for intimate dining. The paneling in the blue dining room of this 1800 house is very special.

The waiter is French and quite knowledgeable about wines. This is important here because wine is Heinrich's hobby. The wine list runs to some 130 choices, including wines from France, Germany, Austria, Italy, Switzerland, California, and New York. Magnums are included and prices run from inexpensive to $65 a bottle. Many of the chateau bottled wines are rare, and the years 1952, 1967 and 1971 are common among the three thousand bottles stored in the inn's wine cellar. Some of the rare vintages have not sold, but Heinrich doesn't mind. "I have enough wine here to last me until I'm eighty," he says.

The inn's four guest rooms, all on the second floor, are nicely furnished, especially the master bedrooms. All rooms open to a second floor living room with plenty of books and magazines.

Open December 20 through March; May 26 to October 15. Closed Monday for dinner. No charge cards, liquor license, no children under six.

ACCOMMODATIONS: MAP $84
                 Dinner $10 - $14

Edson Hill Manor

Edson Hill Road
STOWE, VERMONT 05672

Telephone: 802-253-7371

Innkeepers: John and Joann Rybak, Owner: Lawrence P. Heath

Stowe is one of New England's premier resort towns, with the abundance of motels and the hustle and bustle that marks vacation areas. How pleasant it is to find this country inn high on a hill away from everything except for a few farms, rolling fields, and woodlands.

Built in 1940 as a gentleman's estate, the manor was designed to resemble the log cabins with cottage-type roofs that are so common in provincial Canada. Hand-hewn beams and old bricks accent the facade. Inside, dark woods, more beams, and wide pine floors create an antique atmosphere.

The inn has fifteen rooms, five with fireplaces and eight with private baths. Six of the rooms are in a separate annex just across the drive from the main building. Several rooms in the main building can be joined to make a suite with a private bath for families and traveling couples. The rooms, with traditional decor, have wall-to-wall carpeting, easy chairs, and both twin and double beds.

Edson Hill has been serving a two- to-three entrée dinner, but they are changing to a more expanded menu, and the dining room will be open to the public by reservation. A dining room treat is salad tossed at the table. Entrées include beef Burgandy with shallot sauce, and chicken schnitzel. A full breakfast is included for house guests and, by request, guests may have dinner and breakfast served in their room. A champagne breakfast is an occasional surprise for guests.

The inn has a large living room with fireplace and Oriental rugs, and there is a small lounge with a bar on the lower level. Adjacent is the patio, where lunch is also served. The inn has a cross-country ski center for guests' use, and during the season a skier's lunch is available. During the summer the ski center becomes the stable, and guests at a discount rate can enjoy miles of countryside trails in the shadow of Mt. Mansfield, Vermont's highest peak.

The inn's spacious lawns are accented with a half-moon-shaped swimming pool and lots of gardens. The inn has fishing rods available for guests who wish to try their luck at the trout pond.

Edson Hill caters to couples, and with its secluded location and fireplaced rooms, we can understand the attraction.

Open all year. Children welcome, but no charge cards or pets. From exit 10 on I-89, follow Route 100 to Stowe village, turn left on Route 108 and about five miles from the village turn right up the long hill to the manor.

ACCOMMODATIONS: *MAP* $96 - $150, December to mid-April, mid-June to late October.
EP The rest of the year with continental breakfast.

Foxfire Inn

STOWE, VERMONT 05672

Telephone: 802-253-8459

Innkeepers: Art and Irene Segreto

Once a Chinese restaurant, Foxfire has for the past seven years been the home of authentic Italian dining in the Green Mountains. Art has called upon his Italian heritage and old family recipes to create a menu that speaks of tradition.

As the menu explains, an Italian meal begins with antipasto (perhaps antipasto salad or linguine with clam sauce), then the first principal course (spaghetti with meatballs and various meat or meatless sauces, or fettuccine Alfredo), followed by a second principal course (eggplant parmigiana or cacciatore, or veal parmigiana.)

115 COUNTRY INNS OF NEW HAMPSHIRE AND VERMONT

To cleanse the palate and finish the meal, try salad, cheese (hot Gorgonzola) and fruit, or a sweet (Italian cheesecake or spumoni).

Trying something from each course as the menu suggests may gild the palate, but the point is that the combinations here are endless and no one should leave the table wishing for just a bit more spaghetti.

Before and after dinner, one can relax in the small bar or use either of two sitting rooms with fireplaces and lots of books and magazines.

Each of the five guest rooms has a private bath and each room is identified by a large letter, the initial of the first name of each member of the family. The inn also has a rustic cabin with two bedrooms and a chalet with four bedrooms. Each unit has a kitchenette.

Breakfast for house guests is served in the lovely garden room, complete with white latticework and lots of plants. It's a perfect spot to start the day and remember last night's dinner, Italian style.

Open all year. Charge cards, liquor license, children. Take exit 10 off I-89 and follow Route 100 to Stowe. The inn is on the right, just north of the village.

ACCOMMODATIONS: Winter   *MAP* $70
                  Summer   *EP* $36 with continental breakfast.

Spruce Pond Inn

STOWE, VERMONT 05672

Telephone: 802-253-4828
Innkeepers: Max and Margaret Holland

People get into the inn business for many reasons and from many backgrounds. Max and Margaret vacationed in Stowe in March 1980, fell in love with the area, and instead of skiing, they looked for real estate. On discovering Spruce Pond Inn, they called the rest of their family back in England, announcing their plans to move to America. For Max, who was a textile manufacturer accustomed to flying about in his own plane, and for the rest of the family, the changes have been dramatic. They all seem well-suited to the innkeeping life, though, and have changes planned for this old inn.

Spruce Pond has a busy restaurant business, offering three meals daily, with lunch served on the patio in season. The dinner menu varies from such traditional American fare as steaks and lamb chops to more continental dishes such as veal Oscar, chateaubriand for two, frog's legs, or rainbow trout marabeau. International coffees are a specialty and by all means try the fried ice cream for dessert.

For breakfast, the menu is equally varied — from ham and eggs for the traditional among us to waffles Romanoff for the more adventuresome.

A recent addition is a full-service bar in the comfortable lounge that encompasses most of the original brick farmhouse. There is a large living room with fireplace, lots of books, and a delightfully sloping floor

The main inn building has eight rooms, all traditionally furnished. All have air conditioning and TV, although the latter offered only one channel. Four rooms have private baths, the other four share two baths. Across the street is a twelve-room motel unit and one-and-a-half-acre Spruce Pond, just brimming with trout and deep enough for swimming, although a new swimming pool is in the works.

Max still retains his contacts in England, and he has even begun a special sportsmen's program to lure his former countrymen over for a bit of fishing and hunting.

Open December through March, May through October. Charge cards, liquor license, children. Pets allowed in motel units. Take exit 10 off I-89 and follow Route 100. The inn is on the left just south of Stowe village.

ACCOMMODATIONS: *MAP* $70 - $90
                 EP $35 - $45

Ten Acres Lodge
Luce Hill Road
STOWE, VERMONT 05672

Telephone: 802-253-7638

Innkeepers: Tom Bryant and Yola Carlough

About two miles outside the village of Stowe, amidst rolling farm lands is this rambling old building. Built as a farmhouse about 1826 and with several later additions, the place was converted to a lodge about 1940. Tom and Yola, who have been here for four years, are only the third owners of the inn.

The antiquity of the place is most evident in the comfortable sitting room with old beams, large sofas and chairs, two fireplaces, and fine antiques. Books, games and magazines are plentiful.

The dining room is set up for intimate dining by

candlelight at small tables. The menu is continental, with fillet of duck, chicken à la Parisienne, sole almandine, and something few inns offer — Ten Acres' version of bouillabaisse. Fish and veal specialties are offered daily and everything is cooked from scratch. Breads, soups, and desserts are homemade, as is roast beef hash for breakfast.

There are twenty-five guest rooms, including two cottages, and two apartments, each with two to three bedrooms, fireplaces, and kitchenettes. All but three rooms have private baths. Although a few of the inn rooms are smaller, each is well appointed, with lovely comforters on the beds. The rooms are pine paneled or wallpapered.

Ten Acres Lodge actually has forty-three acres of land with spacious lawns, huge old maple trees, a swimming pool, and tennis court. On the warm day we visited, farmers were haying the nearby fields, and we could just imagine a sparkling white winter afternoon and the chance to slide across those same hillsides on a pair of touring skis.

Open June through October, December to mid-April. Charge cards, liquor license, children. Pets in cottages only. Take exit 10 off I-89 and follow Route 100 to Stowe village. Take a left on Route 108, then turn left on Luce Hill Road about two miles from the village.

ACCOMMODATIONS: Winter *MAP* $100
Summer *EP* $44 - $50
Dinner $8 - $16

Echo Lake Inn
Route 100
TYSON, VERMONT

Mail Address: Box 142, Ludlow, Vermont 05149

Telephone: 802-228-8602

Innkeepers: Mark, Jo, and the Brown Family

Echo Lake is just a few steps from this inn, and the Browns have a private beach plus a large dock with rowboats, canoes, and sailboats for the guests' use. Beside the inn is a large ceramic heated pool with bar and bath house.

The main portion of the inn was built in 1860 and there have been several additions. When the Browns came here three years ago from Pittsburgh, they redecorated the old building and bought Hitchcock furniture for each room. The inn has twenty-one rooms, four with private baths and the others sharing one bath for each two rooms, plus four hall baths. On the fourth floor are five family suites with bunk beds and space for six to eight people. *EP* rates in the bunk rooms are $15.

The large kitchen serves three meals daily — all open to the public — during the summer and foliage season, two meals daily in winter. The varied dinner menu includes steaks, fresh fish, and a few gourmet items such as chicken Cordon Bleu. Breads and pies are made daily at the inn. Mrs. Calvin Coolidge, who lived in nearby Plymouth, was a regular Sunday dinner guest for years.

The large living room has both a fireplace and a grand piano. For more varied entertainment there is a cocktail lounge and game room in the basement.

The inn is popular with skiers, and we noticed a number of ice-fishing shanties on the lake. In summer the place is more relaxed, and we can just imagine an afternoon on the long front porch watching the sunset from an old red rocker.

Open all year. Liquor license, charge cards, inquire about pets. From north of Ludlow, follow Route 100 to the large white inn.

ACCOMMODATIONS: *MAP* $58 - $74
                 EP also available

Knoll Farm Country Inn

Bragg Hill Road
WAITSFIELD, VERMONT 05783

Telephone: 802-496-3939

Innkeepers: Bill and Ann Day Heinzerling

Hosts: The Horner Family

Knoll Farm has one of the best views in the state, but the real beauty of this place lies in the homelike atmosphere created by the Heinzerlings and the Horners.

Ann and her late husband Frank Day started this inn in 1957, but the accent here is on the word *farm*. Not a fancy inn, this is a farmhouse with four rooms sharing three baths. The rooms can accommodate up to twelve people and one room has a beautiful old four-poster that has been in the family since the 1840s and is one of the most comfortable beds we have slept in.

The meals are typical home-cooked Vermont-style, with one-entrée menus and complimentary wine. The vegetables are farm grown and so is the beef and pork. Knoll Farm bacon and sausage are part of the ample breakfasts. Guests are called to dinner by the ringing of bells given by a former guest, Kim Novak. The innkeepers often dine with their guests.

Situated high on a hill overlooking the Sugarbush ski areas, the farm is surrounded by pastures with plenty of room for sliding and ski touring. During the summer, the hillsides are pastures for Scottish Highland cattle, a dairy cow or two, and saddle horses. Guests will also enjoy the dogs, cats, pigs, and other farm animals.

Ann, who leads the winter sliding parties, takes guests riding daily in the summer. In season there also are sleigh and carriage rides. Guests, who often help with haying, weeding the garden, or shelling the peas, may cool off with a swim in the farm pond.

Knoll Farm is enjoyable in any season, but summer is great, especially for family groups. With only four rooms and lots of repeat customers, advance reservations are a must.

Open all year except the months of April and November. BYOB, children over 6. Following Route 100 north toward Waitsfield, turn left a few feet past the intersection with Route 17. The inn is about a half-mile up the steep hill on the left.

ACCOMMODATIONS: *MAP* $56

Millbrook Inn
RFD Box 62, Route 17
WAITSFIELD, VERMONT 05673

Telephone: 802-496-2405

Innkeepers: Joan and Thom Gorman

How many small Vermont country inns feature East Indian dishes on their menu we don't know, but Millbrook does. The Gormans were New York textbook editors who moved north seeking a different way of life. Since they would be the inn's only employees, they knew their menu would have to be something two people could handle. Indian food met their requirement, and since they also made their own pasta, the menu also includes many pasta-based dishes.

How does the menu read? Well, begin with Bhopla Sarvo, a mild curried squash and mushroom soup; then for the main dish try Badami Roghan Josh. This has lamb in a sauce of cardamon, cumin, coriander, coconut, almonds, ginger, tomatoes, and yogurt. Select from a variety of Indian cooked vegetables including cauliflower, spinach, green beans, lentils, and cucumber. The menu also includes non-Indian veal and chicken dishes. Most of the inn's vegetables come from the huge garden they maintain each summer.

Both owners can cook the entire menu, although Joan is usually the waitress while Thom handles the actual cooking each evening. The dining room is open to the public, but reservations are required.

The inn itself is nicely decorated with lots of period furnishings, especially the beds. An old Glenwood woodstove and two fireplaces add to the cozy atmosphere in the winter. A cross-country ski trail from the inn connects with the large complex maintained by the Tucker Hill Ski Touring Center.

Open all year. Charge cards, beer and wine license, no infants in winter. From Route 100 in Waitsfield, follow Route 17 to the inn on the left.

ACCOMMODATIONS: MAP $64 - $68
 EP $36 - $40
 Dinner $7 - $11

Mountain View Inn
Route 17, RFD Box 69
WAITSFIELD, VERMONT 05673

Telephone: 802-496-2426

Innkeepers: Fred and Suzy Spencer

Built about 1830, this old farmhouse has been an inn since about 1948. The Spencers bought it three years ago after Fred, who had been managing a large inn in the valley, got weary of catering to large groups. Mountain View has only four rooms, three sharing two baths. The other, "The Honeymoon Suite," has a private bath and a reproduction canopy bed made by Fred. The other beds and the furnishings are old and Suzy has made quilts for each bed.

Family-style meals are served twice daily on the antique harvest table. Both Spencers prepare the meals, which feature fresh breads daily, hot soups in winter, and home-grown vegetables.

Dinner is served about 6 P.M., but guests vote each evening to set the breakfast hour: the majority rules. German apple pancakes are a breakfast specialty.

Cross-country trails start behind the house and Fred gives tips on off-the-beaten-path ski tours. There's a nice woodstove for cozy winter evenings, but the heat for the entire house is produced by a new wood furnace installed by Fred. Ask him about it.

Open all year. BYOB. From Route 100 in Waitsfield, follow Route 17 to the inn on the right.

ACCOMMODATIONS: *MAP* $60 - $70

Tucker Hill Lodge
Route 17, RFD 1, Box 147
WAITSFIELD, VERMONT 05673

Telephone: 802-496-3983

Innkeepers: Zeke and Emily Church

A ski lodge since 1947, Tucker Hill has been transformed by Zeke and Emily into a comfortable, somewhat sophisticated country inn and restaurant serving the public year-round.

There's a small but cozy living room with fireplace, a well-appointed dining room with contemporary art and photographs on the walls, plus a relaxing barnboard-paneled bar on the lower level.

The twenty rooms (seven with full baths, three with half baths) have a variety of double, twin, and bunk beds so a room or two can accommodate most any size of family. The guest room decor is comfortable New England and features handmade quilts.

The restaurant is one of the most popular in the Mad River valley, serving a variety of gourmet meals by candlelight. Fish is a specialty, and the menu includes filet of striped bass with sea scallops and cucumbers, filet of sole with shrimp and leeks, and papillote of salmon with julienne of vegetables. Steak, veal, chicken, and vegetarian dishes complete the menu, which changes regularly. The lengthy wine list should satisfy the most demanding connoisseur. A cross-country ski lunch is served in season.

Just a few steps from the lodge is the Tucker Hill Ski Touring Center with full rental equipment and the beginning of sixty miles of marked trails. Three downhill ski areas are only a few miles away. Summer guests may use the pool and tennis courts. The special winter adventure package will keep anyone busy and happy.

Open all year. Credit cards, liquor license. From Route 100 at Waitsfield, follow Route 17 to the inn on the left.

ACCOMMODATIONS: *MAP* $68 - $84

Inn at Weathersfield
Route 106
WEATHERSFIELD, VERMONT 05151

Telephone: 802-263-9217

Innkeepers: Mary Louise and Ron Thorburn

The Thorburns bought this rambling old building in 1979 and have created an unforgettable inn. They spent most of a year restoring the structure, and for six months prior to that time, they scoured Ohio (where they were living) for antiques to furnish the inn.

The result is an old-fashioned appearance that exudes New England hospitality. Start with the seven guest rooms, all furnished with antiques, some with canopy beds and crocheted tops, all with private baths, and most with a working fireplace. Beds have electric sheets so they are cozy and warm when you are ready to turn in for the night. You'll also find the covers turned down and a bit of candy on the pillow. On request, breakfast in bed is provided.

Afternoon tea is served in the keeping room or in the library. There is a collection of some twenty-five hundred books, many of them rare. Ron also used to be in the game business and he has forty to fifty games, some prototypes, but others are well-known. All are for the guests to enjoy, and there are chess sets galore.

Mary Louise is the chef, and she cooks everything to order, so plan for a leisurely meal. About seven entrées are offered nightly, and they include chicken Weathersfield, prepared with a glaze of locally produced cider jelly, beef Wellington, several veal dishes, or a French cassoulet — peasant-style meal with goose, bratwurst, filet of beef and vegetables. A soufflé is offered at each meal, and in the continental style, the salad is served after the entrée. All vegetables are steamed.

A variety of hot and cold soups and four to five desserts round out the changing menu. The kitchen woodstove is used for cooking and to heat the kitchen.

The dining room, a converted carriage house with massive beams and a large stone fireplace, has the book collection and a piano that Ron plays during dinner.

The innkeepers have prepared several maps listing suggestions for day trips, and nearby are craft and antique shops, historical sites and covered bridges.

Part of this inn was built in the 1790s and it has been added to over the years. The Georgian columns in front give the place a Southern influence, but the atmosphere is pure New England. And since the inn used to be a stagecoach stop, it is appropriate that along with several bike tours, both horse and carriage groups visit the inn, which has a paddock and several horse stalls.

Open all year. Liquor license, well-behaved children over 8, no pets except horses by advance notice. From exit 8 on I-91, follow Route 131 then turn left on Route 106 and go through the village of Perkinsville to the inn.

ACCOMMODATIONS: B & B and High English Tea $50 - $55
Dinner $10 - $15 served Tuesday through Saturday

Grandmother's House

River Road

WEST ARLINGTON, VERMONT 05250

Telephone: 802-375-2328

Innkeeper: Grandmother (Mrs. Walter Finney)

"This is grandmother's house," Mrs. Finney will tell you, and she treats all guests as if they were family members who have come for the weekend. This inn was and is her home. When her husband died in 1969, she wanted to earn some extra income but didn't want a full-time job. Entertaining friends and her husband's business associates had been regular events for Grandmother, so running a small inn was not that much of a change.

There are four bedrooms, but when honeymooners are staying here Mrs. Finney reserves one as a "mad" room. She only likes to have six guests at any one time. Furnishings are antiques including the four-poster and canopy beds.

Grandmother cooks dinner and serves family style. She sits at the head of the table and eats with the guests. She describes the one-entrée meal as typical of "Grandmother's Sunday best." She'll try to accommodate dietary requirements, and if someone has a special request for dinner, she'll try to meet it. Breakfast is New England style, with eggs, hot cereals, and pancakes.

Meals are not open to the public, and don't you dare come without a reservation. That's something you wouldn't do to your own grandmother. Granddaughter Wendy lives nearby and helps on weekends.

As if Grandmother and her 1792 house weren't special enough, you get to her house by driving across the famed Battenkill River through a red covered bridge, past the church, and straight ahead to her driveway. Mrs. Finney has a tennis court, and there is swimming under the bridge and trout fishing in the Battenkill. Her living room, like most grandmother's houses, has plenty of books and games as well as a piano.

Grandmother only advertised once, ten years ago. Most of her guests come back regularly, and if you need a grandmother, she is more than happy to comply.

Open almost all year. No credit cards, children under 5 for free. River Road parallels Route 313 west of Arlington Village. Just turn by the covered bridge.

ACCOMMODATIONS: MAP $80

The Inn at Saw Mill Farm

Box 8, Route 100
WEST DOVER, VERMONT 05356

Telephone: 802-474-8131

Innkeepers: Ione, Brill, and Rodney Williams

Almost on a whim, the Williams family bought an old farm fourteen years ago. Then, they wondered what to do with it. Eventually they decided to turn the barn into an inn and architect Rodney, using the old beams and boards to advantage, created an imaginative structure. Ione applied her interior decorating skills to furnish the place with antiques and color-coordinated bedrooms.

The accommodations vary and all rooms are luxurious. There are twenty rooms, each with private bath. The master bedrooms are larger, with double vanities in the bathrooms. There are six two-room suites with fireplaces. Each room has matching curtains and wallpaper, fine linens and thick towels, easy chairs, and antique beds. Some rooms are in remodeled outbuildings.

Ione cooked for the first five years, and when her son Brill, a graduate engineer, became interested in the inn, he asked to learn how to cook. For the past eight years he has been the chef.

The decorator's touch is again evident in the dining room. Plates, wallpaper, and even the waitresses' uniforms are coordinated in pink. One wall of the dining room is a greenhouse with a variety of plants. Service is excellent, with several entrées including rack of lamb, chateaubriand, braised duck sliced or flamed at the table.

The cuisine is continental, offering such appetizers as imported caviar and escargot Bourguignonne. Entrées include some unusual specialties: chicken breast in a white wine sauce with black olives, medallions of pork tenderloin with a sauce of cognac, cream and walnuts, sweetbreads, rack of lamb, roast duck au poivre vert, and a Spanish shrimp which is the chef's invention. Desserts add calories just by reading the menu!

The inn has a pool and tennis courts. Mount Snow is just up the road, but many guests come here simply to relax and enjoy the rooms and the dinner.

A television lounge with lots of easy chairs and lots of books is on the top floor of the inn. The main common room decorated with prints and farm tool antiques on the walls is near the dining room and has a huge fireplace. Ione was also in the antique business, and many of her wares — including some lovely copper pieces — were incorporated as part of the decor.

The Inn at Saw Mill Farm is not inexpensive, but prices are relative. For a special weekend, or to celebrate a quiet anniversary, the price here is worth every penny.

Closed December 1 - 18. No charge cards. Children 12 and over, liquor license. Located right on Route 100 north of Wilmington.

ACCOMMODATIONS: *MAP* $110 - $170

West Dover Inn

Route 100

WEST DOVER, VERMONT 05356

Telephone: 802-464-5207

Innkeepers: Alice O'Toole, Walter and Joan Rosenthal

West Dover Inn began as a stagecoach stop in 1846 and has been an inn for many years. The current innkeepers took over about a year ago, moving up from New York where Alice and Joan were nurses and Walter was retired.

Two of the eleven rooms have private baths, and the remainder of the rooms share five hall baths. Most of the furnishings are antiques, with both twin and double beds. The third floor has three dorms, used mainly in the winter for skiers. The wide pine floors are nicely finished.

The menu is varied and everything is freshly prepared by Alice, including the salad dressings and desserts. Barnyard barbecue (chicken and pork baked in a tangy sauce), shrimp scampi, and beef Burgandy are among the specialties.

The dining room, seating thirty-two and open to the public, is brightly furnished and has large windows with views across the Vermont countryside.

Trails from the nearby Sitzmark cross-country center pass the inn and Mt. Snow is just up the road. Lunch is served to skiers in season.

West Dover is just a village, and the inn with its tall front columns is a local landmark.

Open June through April. Charge cards, liquor license.

ACCOMMODATIONS: *MAP* $60 - $78
                 EP $40 - $48

The Darling Family Inn
Route 100
WESTON, VERMONT 05161

Telephone: 802-824-3223

Innkeepers: Chapin and Joan Darling

An inn for the past twenty-five years, this 150-year-old dwelling on the outskirts of the village of Weston was purchased in September 1980 by the Darlings. Their renovations began immediately and have been extensive. The inn now offers five attractive rooms, one with private bath and the other four sharing two hall baths. One large room has a canopy bed, and in all rooms lovely antiques are matched with handmade quilts.

When it comes time to end the day, you'll find your bed linen turned down. Beside the bed will be fresh-baked cookies or brownies and fresh fruit. Still to be renovated are two attic rooms that will have exposed beams. Two housekeeping cottages are also available.

There's lovely stenciling in the hallway, and breakfast is usually served in the living room before the flames of the Defiant woodstove. Breakfast, dinner, and pack lunches are available by request.

The inn has a pool and sits a bit off the road, surrounded by rolling hills. Plenty of ski-touring opportunities are nearby, and in the summer Weston has a playhouse and lots of shops including a most authentic country store (the day we stopped by, the clerk and customers were playing dominos on the counter). The singing monks of the Weston Priory also welcome visitors for regular services.

Open daily. Charge cards, BYOB, children under 8 and pets in cottages only. Located on Route 100, a half-mile north of Weston village green.

ACCOMMODATIONS: $30 - $42 with continental breakfast
Full country breakfast $3.50
Dinner by request $8 - $15
Cottage rates $42 - $47

The Inn at Weston
Route 100
WESTON, VERMONT 05161

Telephone: 802-824-5804

Innkeepers: Stu and Sue Douglas

Just a few steps from the picturesque village green, The Inn at Weston offers a comfortable combination of good food and congenial atmosphere. Sue and Stu worked for a nearby inn before taking over this business eight years ago.

Sue's cooking has earned the inn a feature in *Gourmet* magazine, and the menu, which is changed daily, covers such continental and New England specialties as veal Provençale, chicken Boursin, and Vermont pork and apple pie. Soups, breads, and desserts are homemade and a variety of vegetarian specialties can be prepared with advance notice. In the winter, afternoon tea is served at 4 P.M. with hot chocolate, coffee, mulled cider, and a few pastries.

The inn is laid out so that guests can pass through the kitchen en route to the dining room from the living rooms. It's always a treat to see a good cook at work, and Sue or the chef are happy to explain the menu. Incidentally, the evening meal is always announced at breakfast so that guests may order. While this gives the kitchen staff plenty of time to plan for meals, it also offers the overnight guest the whole day to anticipate dinner.

Adjacent to the dining room, in a remodeled hay barn complete with stone fireplace, is a small bar and game room. Here, veggies, crackers, and dip are provided before dinner, and later in the evening guests get to know each other over board and card games.

Of the inn's thirteen rooms, six have private baths. The rooms are comfortable and varied in size and furnishings. There is an apartment for large families.

The inn is popular with winter skiers and summer playgoers who can walk to the Weston Playhouse.

Open mid-May to November 1st, December 15 through Easter. Liquor license, no charge cards. In Weston village right on Route 100.

ACCOMMODATIONS: *MAP* (Winter) $72 - $88
                  MAP (Summer) $64 - $84

Windham Hill Farm
Off Route 30
WEST TOWNSHEND, VERMONT 05359

Telephone: 802-874-4080

Innkeepers: Jim and Betty Seagers

This 1825 brick farmhouse has been an inn for eighteen years. Situated 500 yards down a winding dirt road and surrounded by 100 acres of countryside open to the guests, the inn offers scenic beauty, country quiet, and the pleasant hospitality of the Seagers.

Canadians who came to Vermont by way of New Jersey, the Seagers were planning to buy a hardware store, but after ten hours of interviews with a broker, they bought this inn. Assisted by three college-age young people, the Seagers provide two meals daily served in their two dining rooms. Guests sit family-style around large tables and meals are served individually from the kitchen. Jim and Betty share in what they call American-style cooking. The five course one-entrée meal at dinner includes soup, salad, vegetables, meat, and dessert. On twenty-four-hour notice the public is welcome for dinner. Breakfast, which is varied and country-style, is for guests only.

Since many guests are repeat customers, Betty keeps a diary of each menu, and when matching it with the guest's last visit, she can serve something different.

The ten guest rooms are named, not numbered, and offer a variety of twin, double, and bunk beds. Eight rooms have private baths and two have private balconies. There are also two dormitory rooms for large families.

After dinner guests can retire to one of three living rooms for game playing, reading, or chatting with the hosts and other guests.

Surrounding hills and fields are perfect for hiking, sliding, cross-country skiing, or just looking down at the rest of Vermont from this high elevation.

Betty loves the children and provides modified meals for them to better fit their appetites and ease parents' pocketbooks. Children are served first, then the adults eat in a more formal dining atmosphere with candlelight.

Open Memorial Day to the end of foliage season, mid-December to the end of skiing. No charge cards, BYOB. From Route 30 turn north at the West Townshend country store. Go up the hill about 1½ miles and turn right at the inn sign on a dirt road.

ACCOMMODATIONS: *MAP* $78 - $90

The Hermitage
Cold Brook Road
WILMINGTON, VERMONT 05363

Telephone: 802-464-3759
Innkeeper: Jim McGovern

Jim McGovern has created one of New England's most interesting inns, so don't come here late in the afternoon for dinner and plan an early departure after breakfast the next day. One should stay here long enough to enjoy the place.

First to be mentioned is Jim himself. "I'm a lucky guy," he says, "I do everything I want to do." "Everything" includes running a major maple-sugaring-operation with 5,000 taps, forty miles of tubing, and production of over 700 gallons of syrup a year. Guests of course are welcome to visit the sugar house and watch the crew at work.

Later in the year, the sugar house becomes a jelly kitchen as Jim turns out some nine thousand jars of preserves, including his own unique maple jelly.

The squawking noise outside the sugar house comes from the pen of wild turkeys raised for the inn, or from the domestic and exotic ducks and geese penned along the brook. Follow the brook downstream to the trout pond and behind the barn is Jim's flock of pheasants, also raised for the inn's table.

Beside the inn is Jim's wine and cheese shop. The wine selection varies from inexpensive to very expensive, heavy on chateau and estate bottled wines from Europe and California. "It's as much a hobby as anything," Jim admits, especially when you look at the inn's wine list and encounter some 550 varieties. Jim personally selects the wine for most diners, and regular guests often call ahead to have their favorite wine ready for their stay.

Jim took over The Hermitage ten years ago, and while his various hobbies keep him busy, the inn is his main business and interest. The menu, which rarely changes, has a variety of continental dishes from shrimp scampi and chicken almandine to frog's legs Provençale and wienerschnitzel. Fresh game is offered in season, including venison. The waiter carefully describes each item on the menu as well as the specials that are offered daily.

After dinner, flaming desserts light up the dining room. Continental coffees also are flamed at the table.

Lunch is served in the summer, usually on the marble patio near the apple orchard. Skiers who use the inn's extensive network of cross-country trails are offered hot soup and sandwiches for lunch. Brunch is served on weekends, accented by Jim's own Bloody Marys and hot buttered rum.

There are five guest rooms in the main inn, each unique and furnished with antiques. The remodeled carriage house has its own living room, four bedrooms, two of which have woodstoves, and a sauna. Brass beds and a four-poster with canopy are especially authentic.

A new addition has seven bedrooms with fireplaces, plus a living room.

Open all year. Credit cards, liquor license. Cold Brook Road is a left turn off Route 100 just north of Wilmington.

ACCOMMODATIONS: MAP $110 - $130

Nutmeg Inn

WILMINGTON, VERMONT 05363

Telephone: 802-464-3351

Innkeepers: Joan and Richard Combes

This 200-year-old, barn-red farmhouse has been an inn since 1957, the last six years under the Combeses' ownership. There are nine rooms, four with private baths. Although the rooms are not large, they are nicely furnished and brightly decorated. The inn caters to family groups in winter, so rooms have double and twin beds. In winter, bunks are added to some rooms.

Joan, who has a food service background, is the dinner cook. Her one-entrée meals are served family-style in the large dining room. Entrées include various roasts, meat loaf, creamed turkey with biscuits, and other home-style cooking. Desserts are Joan's specialty. Richard prepares the full country-style breakfasts.

The old carriage house has been remodeled as the large common room with fireplace, bar, lots of easy chairs, board games, and a piano.

Open Memorial Day to November; mid-December to April. No charge cards, BYOB, children 9 and over. Located just outside the village of Wilmington on Route 9.

ACCOMMODATIONS: *MAP* $60 - $70
MAP (fall) $45 - $48
B & B (summer) $37 per room

The Red Shutters Inn

Box 84, Route 9
WILMINGTON, VERMONT 05363

Telephone: 802-464-3768

Innkeepers: Charles Jones and Loretta Klutsch

Located on a hill just outside the village of Wilmington, the Red Shutters Inn was built in 1895 and has been an inn for a number of years. The current innkeepers, who have been in charge for about a year, have extensive restaurant backgrounds. Charles is the chef and his menu features what he calls "international and imaginative cuisine."

Appetizers include stuffed mushrooms with cheese and herbs, shrimp with garlic sauce, and cream of mushroom soup. Entrées, usually served with three vegetables, are prepared to order and diners are urged to allow two hours to enjoy their meal. Fish is a specialty, featuring scallops, shrimp, trout, and swordfish. Also offered are Veal Picatta, pork tenderloin sautéed with mushrooms, chicken Cordon Bleu, and boneless club steak. The menu does change periodically. The wine list has imported and California selections. Reservations are requested for dinner.

The dining room, with pine paneling and a fireplace, has red decor to match the shutters that give the inn its name. There are also fireplaces in the sitting room and lounge.

The inn has five rooms, all with double beds and mostly furnished with older or antique pieces. All rooms are freshly decorated and have private baths.

Open all year; restaurant closed Monday and Tuesday, except holidays. Charge cards, liquor license, children over 18 only. Located on Route 9, at the west end of Wilmington village.

ACCOMMODATIONS: B & B $48
　　　　　　　　　Dinner $9 - $12

The White House

Route 9

WILMINGTON, VERMONT 05363

Telephone: 802-464-2135

Innkeeper: Bob Grinold

About four years ago, Bob Grinold, who had been the local town manager and was then a contractor specializing in renovations, was asked by a client to look over this old building to see what work needed to be done. The client decided not to tackle the project, but Bob was excited by the place, bought it, and became an innkeeper.

The imposing Colonial Revival mansion was built in 1915 as a summer home for a wealthy lumberman. Its location high on a hill overlooking the village gives the place a commanding view and an image not unlike a more famous White House a few hundred miles to the south.

Rooms on the main floor, from the entrance hallway to the dining room with its mahogany paneling and fireplace, are large and richly detailed, typical of the era in which the building was constructed. The living room has another of the inn's eight fireplaces.

Three of the inn's twelve guest rooms have fireplaces, and two rooms also have balconies perfectly situated to watch the sun setting over the Green Mountains. Four small rooms, remodeled from the old servants' quarters, share one bath, but the other eight rooms are large, with private baths featuring large deep tubs. The rooms are freshly wallpapered and have beautiful hardwood floors.

The inn's front patio has been renovated to make space for the bar-lounge which boasts lots of glass and a woodstove in winter.

The dinner menu includes a variety of chicken, veal, and fish. Duck a l'Orange (with the rib cage removed at the table) is a house specialty. Frogs' legs, lamb chops, and brook trout are also featured.

For Sunday brunch, a White House specialty is Swiss apple pancakes with sour cream. Eggs Benedict and corned beef hash with poached eggs are other brunch dishes as well as the more substantial coq au vin and tenderloin tips.

Winter guests use the inn's ski touring center complete with rental and sales shop and 23-km of groomed trails. A formal garden with roses and brick walks accents the grounds in summer. There are lawn games and a sixty-foot swimming pool.

Season is from May through March, and no dinners are served on Monday; Charge cards, liquor license. Located on Route 9, just east of Wilmington Village.

ACCOMMODATIONS: *MAP* $70 - $125

New England Inn
41 Pleasant Street
WOODSTOCK, VERMONT 05091

Telephone: 802-457-9804

Innkeepers: Bob and Sally Reilly

Built in 1899 as part of a country estate, this village inn has been restored to the Victorian period. Rich oak woodwork abounds and in the cozy tavern, leaded-glass windows, a brass rail, and oak bar reinforce the image of the past. Elsewhere (especially in the dining room) are elaborate fireplaces, tin ceilings, and oak wainscoting.

There are nine guest rooms, two with private baths, one with a half bath. Two hall baths serve the other seven rooms, although five of these rooms have sinks. Many of the furnishings are antiques and the rooms have extra chairs. Beds are doubles, twins, and one king-size.

Bob, who had previously managed restaurants, is the chef. Rack of lamb, duck flambé with cognac and orange sauce, capon sautéed in fresh ginger and garlic butter with wild rice are among the entrées. Fish and veal dishes vary daily. The dining room has small tables enhanced by candlelight for intimate dining. Rugs, fireplace, and chandeliers impart more Victoriana. Dinner is served on the porch in warm weather. Breakfast is diverse and is offered daily, except weekends only during slow periods.

With its many art galleries, antiques, stores, and craft shops, Woodstock is becoming a very popular summer destination for vacationers. The New England Inn is an alternative for people who want to enjoy this village and stay in an interesting hostelry.

Open all year except for a short time in both April and November. Charge cards, liquor license. Located just west of Woodstock Village on Route 4. Take exit 1 off I-89.

ACCOMMODATIONS: *EP* $20 - $30
                  Dinner $8 - $15

INDEX OF INNS

NEW HAMPSHIRE

Back Side Inn, The Goshen	36	Lovett's by Lafayette Brook	
Beal House Inn Littleton	63	Franconia	30
Bernerhof Inn and Restaurant, The		Lyme Inn, The Lyme	67
Glen	33	Maplehurst Inn Antrim	5
Birchwood Inn Temple	107	Martin Hill Inn Portsmouth	88
Bradford Inn, The Bradford	7	Monadnock Inn, The Jaffrey Center	61
Christmas Farm Inn Jackson	50	New England Inn, The Intervale	45
Colby Hill Inn Henniker	41	New London Inn New London	74
Corner House Inn, The Center		Palmer House Inn Eaton Center	19
Sandwich	13	Pasquaney Inn Bridgewater	9
Cranmore Mountain Lodge North		Philbrook Farm Inn Shelburne	90
Conway	80	Pitcher Mountain Inn Stoddard	
Dana Place Inn Jackson	52	Center	96
Darby Field Inn Conway	17	Pleasant Lake Inn New London	76
Dexter's Inn Sunapee	101	Ram in the Thicket, The Milford	69
Edencroft Manor Littleton	65	Rock House Mountain Farm Eaton	
Fitzwilliam Inn Fitzwilliam	23	Center	21
Follansbee Inn North Sutton	84	Snowvillage Inn Snowville	93
Hide-Away Lodge New London	71	Staffords-in-the-Fields Chocorua	15
Holiday Inn Intervale	43	Stonehurst Manor North Conway	82
Homestead, The Sugar Hill	98	Sunset Hill House Sugar Hill	103
Horse and Hound Inn, The		Tamworth Inn Tamworth	105
Franconia	28	Thorn Hill Lodge Jackson Village	57
Indian Shutters Inn North		Tuckerman's Inn and Tavern	
Charlestown	78	Intervale	48
Inn at Christian Shore, The		Village Guest House, The Campton	
Portsmouth	86	Village	11
Inn at Crotched Mountain		Whitneys' Village Inn Jackson	54
Francestown	26	Wildcat Inn and Tavern Jackson	
John Hancock Inn Hancock	38	Village	59

VERMONT

Arlington Inn Arlington Village	115	Blueberry Hill Goshen	145
Barrows House Dorset	134	Camel Hump View Farm Moretown	185
Birch Hill Inn Manchester	171	Castle Inn Proctorsville	195
Black Lantern Inn Montgomery		Chester Inn Chester	123
Village	183	Chipman Inn, The Ripton Village	203

∞ 257 ∞

115 COUNTRY INNS OF NEW HAMPSHIRE AND VERMONT

Churchill House Inn Brandon	117	**Okemo Lantern Lodge** Proctorsville	199
Craftsbury Inn, The Craftsbury	127	**Old Cutter Inn, The** East Burke	140
Darling Family Inn, The Weston	240	**Old Newfane Inn** Newfane	187
Dorset Inn Dorset	136	**Old Tavern at Grafton, The** Grafton	147
Echo Lake Inn Tyson	220	**Quechee Inn at Marshland** Quechee	201
Edson Hill Manor Stowe	211	**Rabbitt Hill Farm** Lower Waterford	165
Foxfire Inn Stowe	214	**Red Clover Inn** Mendon	179
Golden Stage Inn, The Proctorsville	197	**Red Shutter Inn, The** Wilmington	251
Governor's Inn, The Ludlow	167	**Reluctant Panther Inn** Manchester Village	177
Grandmother's House West Arlington	233	**Salt Ash Inn** Plymouth Union	193
Hermitage, The Wilmington	246	**Saxtons River Inn** Saxtons River	205
Inn at Manchester, The Manchester	173	**Shrewsbury Inn** Cuttingsville	132
Inn at Mt. Ascutney, The Brownsville	121	**Spruce Pond Inn** Stowe	216
Inn at Norwich Norwich	191	**Stone House Inn** North Thetford	189
Inn at Saw Mill Farm, The West Dover	235	**Ten Acres Lodge** Stowe	218
Inn at Weathersfield Weathersfield	230	**Three Clock Inn** South Londonderry	209
Inn at Weston, The Weston	242	**Three Mountain Inn** Jamaica Village	152
Inn on the Common, The Craftsbury Common	129	**Tucker Hill Lodge** Waitsfield	228
Jay Village Inn Jay	154	**Tulip Tree Inn** Chittenden	125
Knoll Farm Country Inn Waitsfield	222	**Vermont Inn, The** Killington	158
Londonderry Inn, The South Londonderry	207	**Village Auberge** Dorset	138
Millbrook Inn Waitsfield	224	**Village Inn, The** Landgrove	163
Middletown Springs Inn, The Middletown Springs	181	**Waybury Inn** East Middlebury	143
Mountain View Inn Waitsfield	226	**West Dover Inn** West Dover	238
Munson 1811 House Manchester	175	**West Mountain Inn** Arlington	113
New England Inn Woodstock	255	**White House, The** Wilmington	253
Nordic Inn Landgrove	160	**Windham Hill Farm** West Townshend	244
Nutmeg Inn Wilmington	249	**Windridge Inn** Jeffersonville	156
October Country Inn, The Bridgewater Corners	119	**Woodchuck Hill Farm** Grafton	150
Okemo Inn Ludlow	169		